Contents

C000010040

Publisher's Note

We hope that you obtain considerable enjoyment from this book; great care has been taken in its preparation. However, changes of landlord and actual closures are sadly not uncommon. Likewise, although at the time of publication all routes followed public rights of way or permitted paths, diversion orders can be made and permissions withdrawn.

We cannot of course be held responsible for such diversion orders and any resultant inaccuracies in the text which result from these or any other changes to the routes nor any damage which might result from walkers trespassing on private property. We are anxious that all details covering the walks and the pubs are kept up to date and would therefore welcome information from readers which would be relevant to future editions.

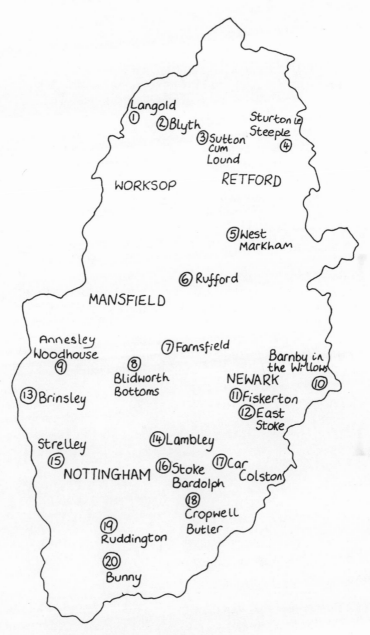

Area map showing locations of the walks.

Introduction

One of my earliest childhood memories is of country walks with my family, usually within spitting distance of the river Trent. We didn't think of ourselves then as hikers, or ramblers, or even walkers. We were just a happy little family, off for an afternoon picnic at Barton, or Colwick Weir, or Hazelford Ferry. The walk was incidental, and we usually took our fishing nets along with us in the hope of netting a few tiddlers.

Later on, I did my walking with the Scouts. Then I caught the bug, and joined a couple of rambling groups. When I got married, and we started our own family, it would have been very easy to abandon walking – if it wasn't for the fact that we were both so committed. So, like Felix the Cat, we kept on walking. But now we took the kids along with us, with rucksacks, flasks, sandwiches and all. The youngsters have all grown up now, but their own enthusiasm for walking (or running, or rock-climbing) has not waned. Now, as grandparents several times over, we still enjoy our regular walks, alone or with our second and third generation. Perhaps our walks are a little shorter in length today, and we tend to buy a pub snack rather more often, instead of carrying a flask and sandwiches every time. Which brings me to the purpose of this book.

The primary aim is to provide a selection of short, easy walks for folk of all ages. Not just the young, not just the mature, but everyone (and not forgetting Rover). Each of the walks is linked to a good, attractive pub where families are welcome and the food and company are the best.

The choice of suitable routes and acceptable pubs is not always an easy task. There are plenty of good walks. There is no shortage of excellent pubs. But the two do not necessarily go together. We hope you will agree with us that this collection meets the very high standards required by our readers, both for the walks themselves, and for the food, drink and hospitality offered by the various licensed houses.

All of the pubs included here welcome families. Most of them have a children's play area, and many have a family room. A number offer a special children's menu and it goes without saying that soft drinks are available, even if the write-up doesn't say so! In addition, just to show that the grandparents are not forgotten, some of the houses provide a senior citizens' menu, on some days at least.

The walks have been chosen, as far as possible, with the triple aims of being 'not too tough, not too long, and not a bit boring'. We have tried to fit in something of particular interest along the way, on every route, be it a country park, a riverside, a battlefield, a piece of industrial architecture or a reminder of one of our local heroes. Several of the pubs, moreover, have their own resident ghost(s)!

The longest walk is 5¾ miles, and the shortest is 2. All are reasonably gentle, because we do not have any really big hills in Nottinghamshire, and one or two are entirely pushchair-friendly. We anticipate that many people will come by car and, where the pub has a car park, you will usually find that – if you ask nicely – you will be allowed to leave your car there while you complete the walk. But where alternative facilities are available, you are encouraged to use them. We recognise, of course, that, even in these affluent times, not everybody can afford to run a car so we have done our best to provide some public transport information where this is available.

And that's enough from me. Enjoy your outings!

Peter Fooks
Spring 1995

1 Langold
The Inn on the Park

This popular family inn, formerly the Miners' Welfare at the now vanished Costhorpe Colliery, has adopted a new role as an essential adjunct of the excellent Langold Country Park. Situated away from the main road, the friendly modern freehouse looks out over busy recreational facilities – in the shape of a bowling green and a cricket field – so there is plenty to interest you while you lunch. Families are welcome here, and the inn provides both a family room and a children's play area, as well as a beer garden.

The inn is open daily, Monday to Saturday, from 11 am through to 11 pm, and on Sundays from noon to 3 pm and 7 pm to 10.30 pm. You can obtain traditional ales here – Stones and Wards – as well as guest beers. The speciality cider is Autumn Gold, and lagers include Carling Black Label and Tennent's Pilsner. The wine list includes both house and table wines. Food is available every lunchtime from 12 noon until 2 pm, with evening catering from 5.30 pm to 9.30 pm in the week, and 7 pm until 9.30 pm on Sundays. Specialities include 'monster steaks', pie of the day, curry, various fish and chicken dishes, pastas and salads, sandwiches and snacks. There is a special children's menu, and an over-60s three course lunch is available Monday to Thursday. Vegetarians are not forgotten.

Telephone: 01909 540311.

How to get there: The Inn lies just off the A60 Worksop to Tickhill road, between Carlton in Lindrick and Oldcotes. Turn off west at the Costhorpe Industrial Estate. The Inn is prominently advertised both at the road junction and on the estate road, where you turn right by the cricket field, and is an easily identified single-storey modern building.

The East Midlands Worksop to Doncaster bus service passes the industrial estate entrance.

Parking: There is no objection to customers parking here while they take a walk, but bear in mind that there is ample parking space just a few steps away in the country park.

Length of the walk: 4 miles. Maps: OS Landranger 120 Mansfield and the Dukeries, Pathfinder 744 Aughton and Carlton in Lindrick (inn GR 584863).

This walk (which, we have to confess, is largely within the boundaries of South Yorkshire!) starts from the Langold Country Park, a splendid recreational facility which will appeal to all the family. There is a magnificent lake, with fishing, boating, wildfowl and circular walks, an outdoor swimming pool and a children's adventure playground. We pass through the park on our outward journey and on our return. But it would be a strange visitor indeed who did not linger here for a while.

The Walk

Starting from the inn, pass around two sides of the bowling green to reach the main (country park) car park. Keep to the left and follow the path straight ahead, waymarked for the lake. This is a grand woodland walk along a broad, firm track – like all those in the park (and most of those on the walk), suitable for pushchairs.

On reaching the lake area, turn right past the ice-cream kiosk, passing through the disabled drivers' car park and on up the approach road to the park gates.

9

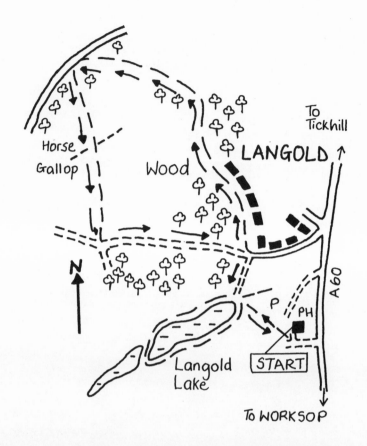

Cross a small parking area and enter Dyscarr Wood, following an extremely clear and well-trodden footpath. Dyscarr Wood is very ancient and has been designated a Site of Special Scientific Interest. The path through the trees is excellent throughout, and is paved in its later stages, but take care not to slip on the sometimes greasy surface.

At the end of the wood, cross a stile and turn left, continuing over open fields along a good farm track. The way leads over two fields before crossing a strip of woodland (Ivy Lodge Plantation) to reach a road, Lamb Lane.

Turn left along the road for a very short distance before re-entering to follow a waymarked bridleway. Strictly speaking, you need not go along the road at all, because there is a connecting

10

The view from Salt Hill Road.

path inside the wood. But this is not, I think, designated a right of way.

Leaving the wood, continue over the fields along a broad hedge-side track, Salt Hill Road. Partway over the fields the track crosses the line of the Firbeck Horse Gallop. There are notices to warn you in time, so there is no great danger, but make sure the coast is clear before you cross and, if horses are approaching, wait until they are past.

The way re-enters woodland and reaches a road. Turn left here and follow the roughly surfaced roadway back to Dyscarr Wood and the country park. From here, the route returns to the inn along the outward route. But before going back there, why not take a stroll around the lake?

Places of Interest nearby
Mr Straw's House, the well-known 'time capsule' owned by the National Trust, can be found at 7 Blyth Grove, Worksop. Visits, by prior arrangement only, can be booked by telephoning 01909 482380.

2 Blyth
The White Swan

The lovely town of Blyth sits on the old Great North Road, a few miles south of Doncaster, and in the far north of the county. The construction of the A1 bypass has proved a blessing, allowing Blyth to retain its traditional charm as a typical, quiet country town. The White Swan, one of the oldest pubs in the area, faces the long green across the ancient main street. The narrow frontage belies the spaciousness of the interior, a fascinating collection of interconnecting rooms, where the pleasing blend of old red brick and timber conveys an impression of age. An unusual feature is a brickbuilt fireplace, standing free in the centre of the bar-room, its hearth raised 2 ft or so above floor-level.

This is a Whitbread house, selling real ales by Castle Eden and Boddingtons, Gaymer's cider on draught, and Stella Artois and Heineken lagers. The opening hours on Monday to Saturday are from 12 noon to 2.30 pm and 7 pm to 11 pm. On Sunday the pub is open from 12 noon to 3 pm and 7 pm to 10.30 pm. Food is provided at all those times, with the exception of Sunday evenings, and an impressive range of main courses includes beef in ale pie, gammon topped with egg or pineapple, fresh haddock, home-made quiche, salads and ploughman's lunch. If you fancy something more filling, you can go for the steak garni – or the chef's special, the Desperate Dan 24 oz T-bone steak with mushrooms, fried tomatoes, onion rings and salad garnish. If you still have room after all that, there is a grand miscellany of sweets, and you can round off your meal with coffee, either straight or speciality. And the snackers are not overlooked, for there is a varied selection of sandwiches on offer, all served with a salad garnish, and either white or brown bread. There is no special family room or children's area, but families are welcome here.

Telephone: 01909 591222.

How to get there: There is easy access from the A1 bypass. Leave the main road either at the A614 junction, if travelling south from Doncaster, or at the Blyth slip road, if coming from the south. The inn is set back from the main street, across the green at the southern end of the town.

A number of bus operators serve Blyth, including East Midland and Retford and District, with services from Doncaster, Bawtry, Worksop, Retford and Gainsborough.

Parking: Parking appears rather limited – from its location by the green, it is not clear whether it is strictly a pub car park, or a public car park! But the landlord does not mind if you leave your car here for an hour or two while you go for a walk.

Length of the walk: 3½ miles. Maps: OS Landranger 120 Mansfield and the Dukeries, Pathfinder 745 East Retford and Blyth (inn GR 625869).

The walk follows a short circular route to Hodsock Priory where, on certain weekends and bank holidays, the gardens are open to visitors. We return to the charming old town of Blyth along quiet estate roads and farm lanes.

The Walk
Follow High Street north from the inn, turning left by the Fourways Hotel onto Sheffield Road. On reaching Park Lodge – the last house

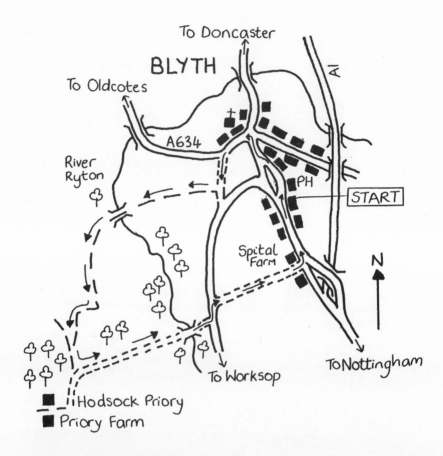

on the left, by the 'No Limit' sign – turn left again, into an avenue of trees. Turn right from the avenue before reaching a pylon, to follow a farm track (no waymark here) on the left of a fragmentary hedge.

At the end of the track, cross a stile and bear left across a green lane to reach a second stile beside a handgate. Over the stile (or through the gate, it doesn't matter), continue up the field on the right of the hedge. Cross another stile, and a footbridge over the river Ryton, then go through a wood to continue once more on the right of the hedge. You will notice that this hedge bends to the right ahead of you. Before reaching the bend, however, turn left to cross through a gap in the hedge. You will see that there is a boundary stone in the dip of the hedge here, with the initials 'GH' cut into it. This is the point at which to cross.

14

The gatehouse at Hodsock.

Through the hedge, turn right through the facing hedge and cross the field on a diagonal line a little to the left of your previous line, making for a gap in the far hedge. On reaching the crossing point (waymarked), pass through and continue over the corner of this next field to reach a broad farm track beside the field edge, and turn left. If there are crops in these two fields, you may find that the path over the first has been diverted a little to reach this track at the field corner.

Follow the farm track past the end of the first field, then turn right through a gap in the hedge. Follow the edge of this next field as directed by the 'CLA' waymark, to reach a stile on the left, partway over the field. Cross this stile and continue over this grass field, passing to the left of a sparse plantation, then bearing right to go through a gateway (double-gated) and follow the cart-track to the Hodsock Priory estate road.

It is a good idea if you can organise your visit to coincide with the opening of the priory gardens to the public – you will need to watch the local press for dates. Early in the spring there is a glorious display of snowdrops in the garden and wood.

Turn left and follow the estate road through to the Worksop road (B6045), passing Guys Plantation and a lodge, and between mature holly hedges, with a wood of tall trees on your right. Cross the river Ryton, and turn left along the public road, taking care to cross over to the right-hand side (and the footpath). Turn right again at the next turning. This is the private drive to Spital Farm, but it is waymarked as a public footpath. Follow the farm road (or, better, the adjacent broad, grassy verge) through to Spital Farm, bearing left with the road, between the buildings, to reach Spital Road. Turn left and follow to the outskirts of Blyth, bearing right at the green to reach the inn.

Places of interest nearby
To the south of Blyth can be found *Clumber Park*, owned by the National Trust, and open daily.

3 Sutton cum Lound
The Gate

The Gate is a cheerful freehouse offering pleasant, friendly service and has traded as a public house for over a century. The interior decor has a pleasing half-timbered effect. There are pictures galore upon the walls, and an interesting collection of bottles. A covered wagon and a horse drawn dray occupy the windowsills.

Opening hours are 11.30 am to 3 pm from Monday to Friday, extended to 5 pm on Saturday, with evening opening from 7 pm to 11 pm. The Sunday hours are noon to 3 pm and 7 pm to 10.30 pm. There is a wide selection of real ales, lagers and wines on offer. Meals and bar snacks are available every lunchtime and evening from Wednesday to Saturday, and at lunchtimes only on Sundays. An impressive menu includes a variety of open sandwiches, salads, quiches, hot sandwiches and sweets. Vegetarian dishes are provided, as also are children's meals. There is no special family room, but families are welcome here, as also are well-behaved dogs.

Telephone: 01777 705992.

How to get there: Sutton is situated about 1 mile north-east of the A638 (Retford to Doncaster) road. Turn off the main road about 1 mile out of Retford or ½ mile from Barnby Moor. The inn stands in the centre of the village, on the corner of Lound Low Road.

Sutton is served by buses from Retford, Bawtry, Doncaster and Worksop, provided variously by East Midland, Road Car, and Retford and District.

Parking: The Gate has its own car park, and you are welcome to leave your vehicle here for the duration of your walk.

Length of the walk: 4 miles. Maps: OS Landranger 120 Mansfield and the Dukeries, Pathfinder 745 East Retford and Blyth (inn GR 682848).

The area around Sutton and Lound has been heavily exploited for sand and gravel, which might suggest a barren landscape. But experience here and elsewhere – at Holme Pierrepont, home to the National Water Sports Centre and at Attenborough, the nature reserve south-west of Nottingham, for instance – has shown that gravel workings are remarkably resilient. Here, in the north of the county, the worked out areas have made an admirable recovery, and now provide excellent recreational facilities. Upon our journey we stroll along the side of one of the resulting attractive lakes, and saunter beside the appropriately named river Idle. And an optional extension offers the opportunity to savour the delights of the Wetlands Waterfowl Reserve.

The Walk

Leaving the inn turn right, following the Lound Low Road. On the first bend, continue straight ahead along a short cul-de-sac, crossing a stile on the right and proceeding along the hedge-side. Bear left at the end of the field and cross a second stile. Go over the next field diagonally, following the overhead wires to reach and cross a footbridge in the far corner. Continue alongside the ditch on the left of the field to reach a farm lane, and turn right.

Follow the farm lane beside a large lake to reach Bell Moor Farm, passing through the gateway (or over the adjacent stile) and bypassing the farm buildings. Cross the field diagonally, still on the farm track, to reach a padlocked gate. There is no proper stile here, but the

short length of metal fence beside the gate appears to serve the same purpose.

Beyond the gate, continue along the farm track until you reach a second gateway. Bear left through the gateway, still on a clear trackway. On reaching a prominent junction, bear right to join and follow a delightful path beside the river Idle.

The Pathfinder map suggests that you might be able to follow a path through to the Barnby Moor road and return thence, by road, to Sutton. But gravel workings are still active in the area, and this does not seem to be a practical proposition. You are recommended to follow the river for about $1/2$ mile and then retrace your steps as far as Bell Moor Farm entrance gate.

On reaching the field gate, pass it by and follow the footpath to the right of this field and the ensuing lake. You will see some wildfowl here – we spotted swans and grebe. Take care along the path, which is 'obstructed' in places with baulks of timber, put there, presumably,

The River Idle at Sutton cum Lound.

to discourage motorbikers. A safer way follows the broader track to the right.

At the end of the path you rejoin the Lound Low Road. The direct route back to the inn turns left here and follows the road, but you are recommended first to turn right for 100 yards or so and visit the Wetlands Waterfowl Reserve and Exotic Bird Park. This is a small but delightful oasis offering a friendly family welcome.

Place of interest nearby
The Wetlands Waterfowl Reserve which can be visited as an optional extension to the walk is open daily, with the exception of Christmas Day.

4 Sturton le Steeple
The Reindeer Inn

The Reindeer is a tastefully modernised, traditional inn in the heart of this pretty little north Nottinghamshire village. The comfortable lounge looks out over the village pond. On warm days you may sit beneath the sunshades on the green, enjoying a snack and a tipple.

The hours of opening at this pleasant freehouse are 12 noon to 3 pm throughout the week, including Sunday. In the evenings it is open from 7 pm to 11 pm on Monday to Saturday and 7 pm to 10.30 pm on Sunday. The real ales include Boddingtons, Eden and Trophy. Meals and bar snacks are provided daily, from 12 noon to 2 pm, and from 7 pm to 10 pm every evening, except Tuesday. The bill of fare includes home-made pies, both steak and Guinness and steak and onion, chicken nuggets and sirloin steak. Among the sweets are such old favourites as spotted dick, jam roly-poly and treacle sponge. The children's menu includes fish fingers, French fries and chip butties. Families are welcome at the Reindeer and there is both a family room and a children's play area.

Telephone: 01427 880298.

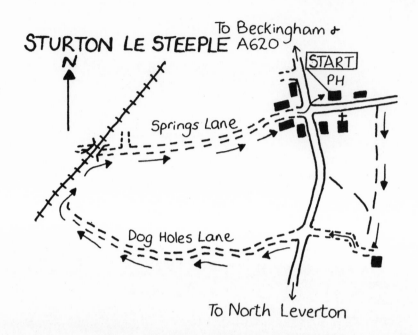

How to get there: The nearest main road to Sturton is the A620 (Retford to Beckingham), a couple or so miles to the north at Bole. Alternatively, the village can be approached on minor roads via North Leverton, from Retford, in the west, or Darlton (on the A57), to the south. The inn is in the centre, near the crossroads and right opposite the church.

Parking: The licensees have no objection to patrons leaving their vehicles in the car park here for an hour or two while they walk.

Length of the walk: 3¼ miles. Maps: OS Landranger 120 Mansfield and the Dukeries, Pathfinder 745 East Retford and Blyth (inn GR 787839).

This is an easy walk for the whole family, young or mature. It is level all the way, and most of the route is along country lanes. Less than 1 mile is on field paths – and they can be avoided, if you prefer, by following the Leverton road for the first ¹/₂ mile, as far as Dog Holes Lane, and completing the walk on farm tracks and lanes. The village of Sturton le Steeple is dominated by the presence, just to the north, of the immense West Burton power station. The great cooling towers are, however, surprisingly unobtrusive.

The Walk

Turn left along Church Street, passing the church and the school. The Pathfinder map shows the footpath as leaving the road just beside the school, but this has been diverted, and you will need to follow the road for some distance until you come to the replacement stile, beside a wooded area, at the end of the field. Cross the stile and follow the edge of this, and the next long field.

Alternatively, you can turn right from the pub and follow the Leverton road for a while, to reach a footpath sign beside a farm gate on the left. Pass through the gap at the side of the gate and cross the field, bearing slightly right, to reach a stile in the far corner of the field – and to meet the path already described.

Cross the stile and continue, still following the edge of the field, with a spinney on your left. The field was cropped when we came but the path was clear – still take care, because the ground may be very uneven. Follow the hedge round to a stile beside a house and turn right along a metalled lane. At the Leverton road turn left, then right again into Dog Holes Lane – a broad, unmetalled farm track.

Follow this lane for about 1 mile. There are wide views from here. The windmill you can see over the fields to the left is North Leverton mill – a working mill which is open, at certain times, to the public.

Stay with the track as it bends to the right, passing to the right of a railway line. This is perhaps the point where you get your best view of the power station – that may sound like a contradiction, but it does have a certain grandeur. It is an interesting exercise to compare it in scale with the far older, but much more elegant, tower of Sturton church, also visible from here.

Bear right again to join and follow Springs Lane, to bring you back to Sturton village.

Preserved windmill at North Leverton.

Places of interest nearby

To the west, just off the A620, can be found the *Clarborough Tunnel Nature Reserve*, run by the Nottinghamshire Wildlife Trust. To the south is the *North Leverton Windmill*, open every afternoon, except Tuesdays, and to the east, the *Littleborough Toll Cottage*. A visit to the *Sundown Kiddies Adventureland and Pets Garden* at nearby Rampton will delight youngsters. It is open daily, except Christmas Day and Boxing Day.

24

5 West Markham
The Royal Oak

This roomy and comfortable inn on the old Great North Road has
been completely renovated in recent years, and provides excellent
facilities and exceptional home cooking in a traditional, friendly
atmosphere. The Royal Oak is situated only $\frac{1}{2}$ mile from the busy
A1 trunk road and is popular with motorists, walkers and locals alike.
It could be described as all things to all people. Families are not just
declared to be welcome – there is a family room and a children's play
area to prove it, not to mention a beer garden and a no-smoking area.
Moreover, dogs, if well-behaved, do not have to be left outside.

The Royal Oak provides both bar snacks and full meals, at
lunchtimes and in the evenings, and a wide-ranging menu includes
home-made meat and potato pie, steakwiches, all-day breakfast,
vegetable lasagne, delicious filled rolls and jacket potatoes, not
forgetting the dish of the day, and a traditional Sunday lunch. There
is a special menu for the under-twelves and another for vegetarians.
If you like a bottle of something to accompany your meal, there is a
comprehensive wine list to choose from. This is a freehouse, offering

25

Marston's bitter, Red Admiral and Riding ales, as well as Foster's and McEwan's lager, and cider on draught. The opening hours are, daily, from 11.30 am to 3 pm and 6 pm to 11 pm, but also, on occasion, for the whole day.

Telephone: 01777 870491.

How to get there: From the A1 trunk road, turn off south, onto the B1164 (Tuxford) road, at the Markham Moor roundabout. The inn is a prominent building, ½ mile on, on the right-hand (western) side of the road.

The Road Car bus service runs between Retford, Tuxford and Ollerton.

Parking: You will be allowed to leave your car here for an hour or two, if you ask first. There is no viable alternative parking area within the area of the walk.

Length of the walk: 2¾ miles. Maps: OS Landranger 120 Mansfield and the Dukeries, Pathfinder 763 Clumber Park and East Markham (inn GR 723732).

The Royal Oak is a pub with no village, being situated on the open road. But this short, circular walk visits two – the quiet little village of Milton, and equally tiny West Markham, where the ancient church is a gem.

The Walk

Leave the road by a waymarked bridleway, directly alongside the south side of the inn. Cross one field and a footbridge, then continue over another very large field, following a broad farm track, which leads into an enclosed lane to reach the village of Milton.

Turn left and follow the road through the village, passing the end of the West Markham road. A short way down this side road, if you choose to explore a little, you will come to the mausoleum built by the 4th Duke of Newcastle as a final resting place for the members of his family, with the intention of replacing the parish church at West Markham.

Continuing along the 'top' road for about ½ mile, pass on your left the Markham Clinton pumping station and carry on to the next turning on the left – a rough farm track. Although there is no signpost

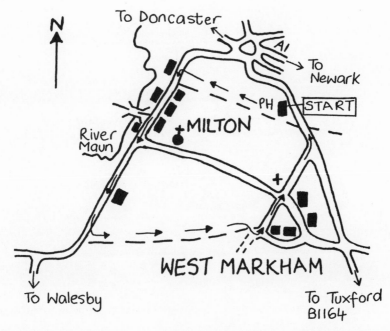

to mark it as such, this is a public bridleway. Curiously enough, there is a footpath sign directly opposite, marking the end of a footpath which, supposedly, runs from opposite the pumping station. But when I tried to follow it, I was thwarted by an impenetrable hedge!

Turn left onto the bridleway, following the right-hand side of the hedge, which will lead you into and along a sunken way. Emerge again onto open fields and thence continue to West Markham.

Turn left at the road to arrive soon at the village church of All Saints. A remarkable little building, it was for many years in a state of neglect, following the Duke of Newcastle's decision to build his own family mausoleum and church 1/2 mile away at Milton. Happily, the locals voted in the present century to reinstate All Saints as the village church – a commendable decision.

The church is a veritable treasure, with both Saxon and Norman elements in its structure. There is a door which is at least 600 years old, a Norman font, a Jacobean pulpit, and several high old oak benches, probably Tudor, not to mention an earthen floor. The bell in the tower, still in use today, dates from the 15th century. Visit the church – and be generous with your donations. This is a tiny parish, and maintenance of this outstanding little house of God a

Spring cleaning at All Saints, West Markham.

daunting task. The sterling efforts made by the small congregation deserve recognition.

Follow the road right and left past the church, then onward to reach the Great North Road and turn left, back to the inn.

Places of interest nearby

A restored windmill, *Longbottoms Mill*, is situated at Great North Road, Tuxford. Telephone 01777 870413 for opening times. To the west, at Haughton, is *The World of Robin Hood*, open daily in summer, and at weekends, school and bank holidays in the winter.

6 Rufford
The Rose Cottage

The Rose Cottage, to be strictly honest, might best be described as a licensed restaurant rather than a pub. However, that would be an over-simplification, for the fact is that this charming modern establishment fully meets both definitions. As an eating house – the sign outside describes it as 'A Family Dining Experience' – it is second to none, but it also boasts an excellent lounge bar, where you may enjoy a drink, while waiting for a table – or just for its own sake, without the need to buy a meal. The Rose Cottage was once just that. A particularly attractive private dwelling on the corner of the Edwinstowe road, which always drew an admiring glance in passing. It has changed its role today, but is no less attractive. The present owners, The Mansfield Brewery Company, have greatly improved and extended the facilities.

The opening hours are from 11 am to 3 pm and 5 pm to 11 pm on Monday to Saturday, and 12 noon to 3 pm and 7 pm to 10.30 pm on Sunday. The range of ales includes Riding and Old Baily. The lagers are Foster's and McEwan's, and Woodpecker cider is on draught.

There is a comprehensive wine list, with red and white house wines, dry, medium and sweet, as well as champagne and sparkling wine, and low alcohol Eisberg. Food is available daily, from 12 noon to 3 pm and 5.30 pm to 9.30 pm in the week, and from 12 noon through to 9 pm on Sunday. The mouth-watering menu includes traditional home-made steak and kidney pie, lasagne bolognaise, chicken tikka masala, a range of steaks, and deep-fried haddock. There are various starters (we particularly recommend the crock pot of soup) and a tempting selection of sweets. Then there are the chef's daily specials, a splendid 'Supper for Two' after 8 pm and a superb Sunday lunch. Vegetarian dishes are available, as well as a very popular children's menu. Certain of the dishes are also served in smaller helpings at a reduced price for the young and the not quite so young. Families are demonstrably welcome in the dining area, and there is a children's play area – and the disabled visitor is not forgotten. In addition, you will find a beer garden, a non-smoking area and an outside barbecue, when the weather is suitable. Well-behaved dogs are not objected to, in the garden area.

Telephone: 01623 822363.

How to get there: The Rose Cottage is situated on the A614 Nottingham to Doncaster road and on the corner of the B6034 Edwinstowe road, 2 miles south of the Ollerton roundabout. It is directly opposite the Rufford Country Park. The East Midlands bus service between Nottingham and Worksop passes the Rose Cottage.

Parking: There is parking at the Rose Cottage, but this is a very popular eating place and it is not a good idea to overstay your welcome, particularly bearing in mind that the country park, where you will be walking, has its own excellent parking facilities. For this reason, the walk is described from the car park on the A614.

Length of the walk: 2 miles, or 2½ miles if you choose to walk right round the lake. Maps: OS Landranger 120 Mansfield and the Dukeries, Pathfinder 780 Ollerton (inn GR 641650).

This walk is wholly within the area of the Rufford Country Park, a deservedly popular spot with visitors from all over Nottinghamshire, and beyond. The basic 2 miles of the detailed route might mislead

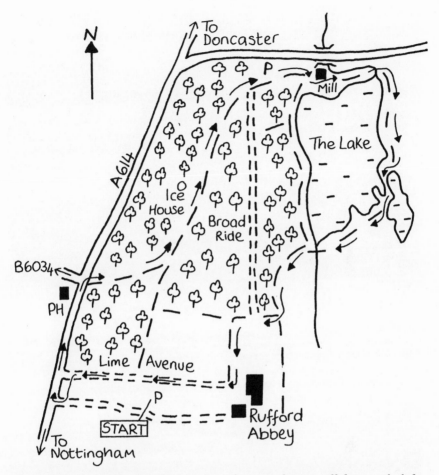

you into supposing that little more than an hour will be needed for the complete circuit. There is so much to see and do, however, that you should allow much more time than that.

The Walk

Leave the car park, join the road and turn right. Pass the Rose Cottage and, immediately opposite the Edwinstowe road, pass through a gap in the fence, following an unmarked footpath through Wilderness Wood. This path, narrow at first, soon broadens out into a well-defined way through glorious woodland. On reaching a T-junction, turn left onto a broad trackway, passing close by the Ice

'Ewe and Man on Bench' in Rufford Country Park.

House. Continue on along the same track, passing the end of Broad Ride, to reach the Wellow road car park.

Follow the right-hand edge of the car park to re-enter the country park by the Wildlife Sanctuary entrance and arrive at the lake. The lake is rich in wildfowl – mallards, coots, waterhens, Canada geese and swans, to name just a few. Turn left at the lake, passing Rufford Mill. You will find an information office here, as well as refreshments and toilets, and various displays and exhibitions are laid on during the season. The lake (and the millstream) are fed by the Rainworth Water, which crosses the Wellow road by a ford here, another source of entertainment for the visitor.

Cross the head of the lake by a long footway and continue around its eastern side. At the foot of the lake the path swings left to pass a field, normally used for the park's flock of sheep. These are Mouflon, said to be the original ancestor of all the modern breeds. The way leads on, past the field, to arrive at the site of Rufford Abbey.

A recommended short extension of the walk – about $\frac{1}{2}$ mile – continues from the foot of the lake along its western side. When nearly back at the mill (soon after passing a row of benches on your left) turn left through the trees to reach the Broad Ride. Turn left and follow this beautiful green avenue through to its end, passing through the hedge at the end to reach the abbey green.

Very little of the original abbey remains, although part of the former monastic buildings was converted into a residence, remaining as such until the present century when, before the County Council took a hand, it fell into serious disrepair. A pleasant hour or two can still be enjoyed here in the craft centre and gardens. There is also an excellent restaurant in the coach house, as well as a bookshop, information office and toilets.

Leave the abbey by Lime Avenue, directly opposite the entrance to the house. There is no direct exit to the road from here now, but a pathway on the left, just before the gate, will lead you to the car park.

Places of interest nearby
Sherwood Forest Country Park and Visitor Centre can be found just a short way to the north-west, at Edwinstowe.

Farnsfield
The Plough Inn

There is no shortage of attractions for the visitor in the Farnsfield area. Whether your taste is for farm centres, butterfly parks, old railway tracks – or good pubs – you are sure to find something here to interest you.

The Plough is a cheerful, friendly 'Mansfield Brewery' house, and the oldest inn in this attractive central Nottinghamshire village – dating back to the 14th century. The interior decor is tasteful, with oak beams and a charming collection of brass and copperware. And the toilets are the cleanest we have seen anywhere! Outside is a delightful, and award-winning, garden with an excellent picnic area and children's swings.

The opening hours are from 11 am to 3 pm on Monday to Friday, extended to 4 pm on Saturday, and from 6 pm to 11 pm in the evenings. Sunday hours are from 12 noon to 3 pm and 7 pm to 10.30 pm. The ales on offer include Old Baily and Riding, or you may choose from a selection of lagers and wines, or cider on draught. Meals and bar snacks are available, lunchtimes only, from

Monday to Saturday, and a tempting menu includes a wide variety of grills, fish and meat dishes, sandwiches and snacks. Patrons may eat their own food in the garden at non-catering times – do ask first. There is no special family room, but families are welcome, as are well-behaved dogs.

Telephone: 01623 882265.

How to get there: Farnsfield is a large village on the unclassified road between Southwell and Rainworth. The usual approach is from the A614 Nottingham to Doncaster road, turning off east at the 'White Post' roundabout. The Plough is towards the eastern end of the village.

Farnsfield is served by buses (East Midland and Road Car) from Mansfield, Newark and Southwell.

Parking: The car park is capacious, and customers are welcome to park for the term of their walk, but, again, please ask.

Length of the walk: 3³/₄ miles. (This can be reduced to a mere 2¹/₄ miles by omitting the Hexgreave estate and following the Southwell Trail – but that would mean missing out on the most enjoyable part of the walk!) Maps: OS Landranger 120 Mansfield and the Dukeries Pathfinder 796 Newark-on-Trent West (inn GR 650565).

We never cease to be amazed at our capacity for finding new delights: they call it serendipity. Until we discovered this walk, we had never heard of Hexgreave, nor its splendid avenue of lime trees. You follow a minor road out of Farnsfield and cross first the Southwell Trail – a former railway now converted to a footpath way. Then over the fields to reach the Hexgreave Estate, where you join the drive, threading the avenue back towards Farnsfield.

The Walk

Leaving the inn, turn left onto Main Street, and left again into Brickyard Lane. This road is initially metalled, but the houses are soon left behind and the way reverts to a rough track and, after passing the former pumping station (now a dwelling) on the left, to a green lane. A little footpath on the left here – well trodden but not too obvious – leads through the hedge to the Southwell Trail. This

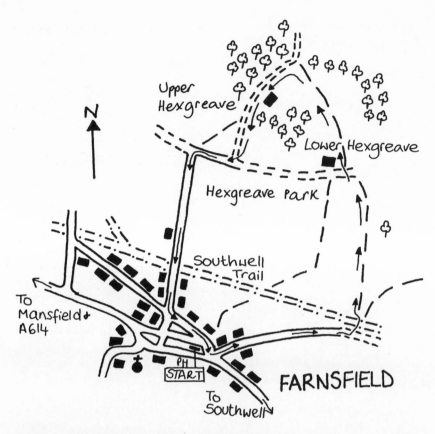

was formerly the Farnsfield to Southwell railway line, but is now a popular walkway.

Cross the trail and follow the hedge-side directly ahead, keeping to the edge of the field to negotiate a double bend. At the end of the hedge continue along the unfenced farm track before you, passing to the left of the Park Plantation and bearing left at a junction of tracks to reach Lower Hexgreave Farm.

At the farm entrance, take a footpath on your right, skirting around the buildings to reach an open field. Bear left a little now to cross the open parkland of Hexgreave. Hexgreave Hall will be visible ahead, against the woods on the left, as you cross the park. You may well find that the grounds are partly cultivated, but signs of the route should normally be visible. The line of the path crosses approximately midway between the trees on either side, passing close

Upper Hexgreave.

to a prominent tall lime tree and continuing on, via a stud farm, to reach a stile leading into a belt of woodland.

Cross the stile,. and a second one, and pass through the wood to reach a good track and turn left, following a beautiful avenue of mature lime trees, and passing the entrance and outbuildings of Hexgreave Hall.

Continue along the avenue for a good ¹/₂ mile to its southern end. A footpath on the right a little way along suggests a short cut, but this offers little advantage, particularly if there is a growing crop in the field, and the exit stile when we came was seriously overgrown.

Turn right at the end of the avenue, then left again at the entrance to Cockett Barn Farm, to follow a straight metalled road. Pass South Lodge and the Southwell Trail and reach the outskirts of Farnsfield.

Turn left along Far Back Lane and follow it through to the inn car park's rear entrance.

Places of interest nearby
White Post Modern Farm Centre, and *Butterflies Pleasure Park*, are both situated at Farnsfield and are open daily.

8 Blidworth Bottoms
The Fox and Hounds

A cosy little pub in a rural setting, the Fox and Hounds was originally a farmhouse but was converted to an inn in the early years of the present century. Not far from Newstead, it is no surprise that the house is reputed to have had associations with the poet Byron. A vast array of pictures decorates the lounge, including paintings of traditional country cottages and the like, as well as snaps of off-road cars. The fireplace is particularly interesting – it now houses an aquarium!

This is a Hardys and Hansons house, and Kimberley hand-pumped ales are sold here, both bitter and mild. Other beverages include Strongbow cider, Heineken lager, and Allouette wines. Lunchtime opening is from 12 noon to 3 pm throughout the week, including Sunday. In the evenings the pub is open on Monday to Saturday from 6 pm to 11 pm, and 7 pm to 11 pm on Sundays. Meals and bar snacks are available every lunchtime, and each evening, except Wednesdays. A comprehensive menu includes home-made steak and kidney pie, chicken and mushroom pie, Cornish pasties, giant-sized

Yorkshire puddings with a choice of fillings, and assorted jacket potatoes. There is a Friday special of fish and chips, and a very popular traditional Sunday lunch. There is also a children's menu. If you are careless enough to arrive when food is not available, you will be allowed to eat your own snack in the excellent garden area. Families are welcome here, as are well-mannered dogs, and there is a family room and a children's play area.

Telephone: 01623 792383.

How to get there: From the A614 Nottingham to Doncaster road, turn off west onto the unclassified Ravenshead and Kirkby-in-Ashfield road, about 3 miles north of the A60/A614 junction. The inn is a little over 1 mile along, directly opposite the Rigg Lane junction.

Parking: There is no objection to patrons leaving their cars here while they go for a walk. It is also worth noting that the woodlands visited in the course of the walk have several access points, each with its own parking area.

Length of the walk: 3 miles (or 4 miles with an optional extension). Maps: OS Landranger 120 Mansfield and the Dukeries, Pathfinder 795 Sutton in Ashfield (inn GR 590548).

No guide to Nottinghamshire's walking country would be complete without a visit to Sherwood Forest. Much of the original forest area has ceased to exist, but some delightful areas of ancient woodland remain alongside the more recent Forestry Commission plantings. This walk is entirely over Commission lands, but the woodland is mixed and the walking pleasant. The main route follows one of the waymarked routes for much of the walk, but an optional extension of 1 mile takes in a section of the Robin Hood Way.

The Walk
Follow Blidworth Lane in a south-easterly direction for ½ mile to reach the Blidworth Bottoms car park and picnic area. Pass the toilet block on your left, following a broad forestry road until you reach a narrower path crossing from right to left and marked with blue and white marker posts. Turn left and follow the marked route, keeping a sharp eye open for the blue and white markers. After a

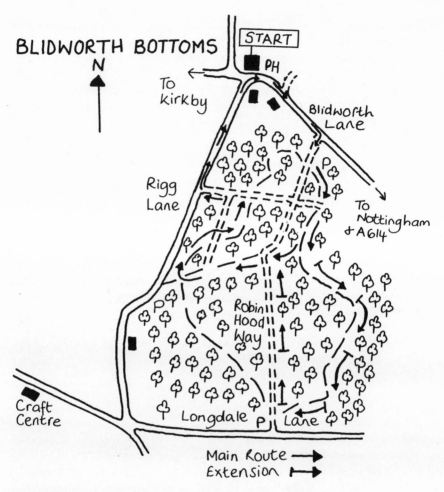

BLIDWORTH BOTTOMS

N

To kirkby

Rigg Lane

START

PH

Blidworth Lane

To Nottingham & A614

P

Robin Hood Way

P

Craft Centre

Longdale P Lane

Main Route ⟶
Extension ⊢⟶

while the path approaches the edge of the woodland, while remaining just within.

Where the path branches, one branch continuing straight ahead, take the rightward branch and re-enter the wood proper, still following the blue/white markers. Soon after this, the two routes diverge, the blue route continuing ahead and the white turning off right along a narrow path through the heart of the wood.

For the optional extension, continue ahead, following the blue markers. After a while, the way leaves the wooded area to follow a sandy track over open, scrubby ground, with wide views over

Path through Blidworth woods.

the surrounding countryside. Pass a seat at a crossing of paths and re-enter the woodlands. After passing close to a power line, you meet a broad forestry road near the Longdale Lane car park. Turn right here, leaving the 'blue route' and joining the Robin Hood Way – one of the county's own long-distance footpaths. The track runs straight for ½ mile in a northerly direction. Climb one steepish hill, then descend a little before climbing again to reach a bend in the track, where a second track crosses right to left. Turn sharp left here (three-quarters of a complete turn) to join the white route as it enters the wood.

For the main route, look out carefully for the branching of the paths, because it is not too obvious – but if the next post you see has only a blue marking, you have missed it! Follow the white markers, taking a well-marked route across the wood. For much of the way you will note that the path parallels a broader track, but the waymarked, narrow way is infinitely better. Keep to this track until you once more meet the blue route, merging from your left. Cross the broad forestry road and reach the Rigg Lane car park.

Pass the car park at its extreme end, bearing right and following the blue and white markers. The path crosses a north/south forestry track before turning left to descend to a second broad track. Turn left now, leaving the waymarked route, and keep straight forward along the horse trail until you emerge onto Rigg Lane. Turn right, back to the inn.

Places of interest nearby
Just south of Blidworth Bottoms, at Longdale Lane, Ravenshead, is the *Longdale Craft Centre and Museum* which is open daily except Christmas Day and Boxing Day, and the *Abbeydale Farm Centre*, open daily. *Papplewick Pumping Station*, just off Longdale Lane, is open Sunday afternoons, April to October inclusive; in steam at bank holidays and certain other weekends throughout the year.

9 Annesley Woodhouse
The General Havelock

The 'Havelock' is a friendly, roomy, estate inn, with a country pub atmosphere. On the fringe of a traditionally working-class area, the house dates back over 100 years, when it formed a part of the old village of Annesley. It stands today in the midst of an estate of modern houses and bungalows. To our shame, we had never heard of General Havelock until we found this pub. A note on the menu reminds us that this man's daring in battle (at the time of the Indian Mutiny) salvaged the pride of the British Army when, but for his bravery and skill in relieving a besieged garrison, events could have brought about a crushing defeat.

The inn belongs to Scottish and Newcastle (Home Brewery), and the range of real ales includes Theakston, plus a regular guest ale. The pub is open from 11.30 am to 3 pm and 7 pm to 11 pm, between Monday and Saturday, and 12 noon to 2.30 pm and 7 pm to 10.30 pm on Sunday. Food is available every day, except Sunday, from 12 noon to 2 pm, and 7 pm to 9 pm in the evening. Main courses include beef and Old Peculier ale pie, chicken Kiev, fillet of plaice or haddock, horseshoe gammon and tomato and basil flan, all served with chipped or jacket potatoes, salad garnish and peas. There is a tempting selection of sweets, and coffee, fresh filter or liqueur, to follow. Light bites include a variety of delicious sandwiches and jacket potatoes, ¼ lb beefburgers, jumbo beef and pork sausages and salad platters. Daily specials are posted up on the blackboard in the bar and a children's menu is also available. Families will feel at ease here, even though there is no special family room. There is a children's play area, however, and a beer garden, and well-behaved dogs are welcome.

Telephone: 01623 752488.

How to get there: If coming via the M1, turn off east at junction 27, to follow the A608. On meeting the A611 Hucknall to Mansfield road, turn left. Turn left again at the next turning, Forest Road, by the Badger Box Inn. Skegby Road is about ¾ mile along on the right.

Parking: The Havelock has a large car park, but please ask the landlord if you want to leave your car here while taking your walk. Alternatively, there is a roomy layby beside the M1/A608 slip road, which directly adjoins the route (partway round).

Length of the Walk: 3¼ miles. Maps: OS Landranger 120 Mansfield and the Dukeries, Pathfinder 795 Sutton in Ashfield (inn GR 498536).

Sandwiched between the traditional coal mining district of Annesley and the M1 'speedway', and with a modern photographic works immediately to the south, it might be supposed that the Annesley Woodhouse area has nothing to offer the seeker after peace and solitude. In fact, none of these features has had quite the impact one might have expected on the natural beauty of the district, which also contains the ancient Annesley Hall and Park. Our route completely circumnavigates the Kodak Works, and passes very close to the motorway, yet neither of these intrudes on the delight of the walk.

The Walk
Follow Skegby Road down to the junction with Forest Road and Salmon Lane and turn right. When opposite Salmon Farm (a

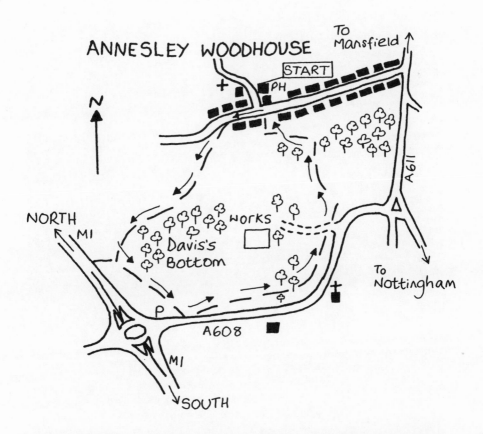

misleading title!) turn left onto a waymarked footpath. Follow the hedge-side down the field until you reach a gap, and here bear right, across this same long field. On the far side, continue down the field, now on the left of the hedge.

At the bottom of the field, cross a stile and carry on over the next field, to reach and cross another stile at the extreme end of a wood. Climb up over this field, making for a clump of trees. Below on the right you will get a view of two large fishponds, where the Cuttail Brook broadens out. On reaching the trees, bear left along the hedge to the top of the field. Pass through a gap in the hedge and cross right to reach a stile between a farm gate and the broken wall of a derelict farm building.

Cross the stile and pass around the building, continuing along the edge of the field to reach a guide post. At this point you obtain

45

View over fields near Davis's Bottom.

your only real view of the traffic speeding by on the M1 – a brief glimpse, because you immediately turn left to follow a good green track, almost to the A608 (the M1 slip road).

A stile crosses here to the slip road, but that is not your route. Instead, follow the track through the hedge on your left, bearing left again at a gate to follow a footpath alongside the hedge. After passing through a brief wooded area, cross an open field, with the low profile of the Kodak building now visible in the dip – Davis's Bottom – on your left. Bear left at a footpath sign to re-enter the woods, keeping to the woodland path over an intervening farm track.

Beyond the woods, cross the Kodak access road and continue round the edge of one field. Cross a farm track and carry straight on along a very well-used, fenced footpath. Follow this path through, ignoring two side turnings, to reach Forest Road. Turn left, and right again into Skegby Road, back to the inn.

Places of interest nearby
Newstead Abbey, just off the A60 Nottingham to Mansfield road is well worth a visit. The grounds are open throughout the year and the house is open daily, April to September.

10 Barnby in the Willows
The Willow Tree Inn

This is the inn that the author has long been looking for – the one that serves tripe and onions! A bright, friendly village pub, the Willow Tree dates back to the 17th century. The focal point of the cheerful lounge is the brick-built bar counter which, with the oak beams and horse brasses, underlines the traditional atmosphere of the place. An amusing addition to the decor here is a framed poem (1951 vintage) extolling the virtues, and otherwise, of the inn and its clientele.

The Willow Tree is a freehouse, offering Bateman, Tetley and Worthington ales, as well as a regular guest ale. The draught cider is Scrumpy Jack, and lagers include Carling, Carlsberg and Holsten. New Zealand wines are a speciality here. The opening hours are from 12 noon to 2.30 pm and 7 pm to 11 pm on Monday to Saturday, and 12 noon to 3 pm and 7 pm to 10.30 pm on Sunday. Food is available here, both snacks and full meals, every day, until half an hour before closing. There is a comprehensive printed menu, as well as a full blackboard listing the daily specials and bar snacks. If tripe and onions is not to your taste, you can try Chinese glazed ribs, game pie, chicken and chips or curry and rice. Then there is a popular two-course lunch (with the option of either starter or sweet) from Monday to Friday. Snacks include beefburgers, cheeseburgers, sandwiches, toasties, ploughman's lunch, and salads. Families are actively catered for here at Barnby, and there is both a family room and a children's play area. There is also a beer garden. Well-behaved dogs are welcome, if on a lead. Bed and breakfast accommodation is available, too.

Telephone: 01636 626613.

How to get there: Using the A17 Newark to Sleaford road, turn off south about 3 miles east of the junction with the A46 and the A1. An alternative, unclassified, road runs from Newark town centre direct to Barnby.

The village is served by buses from Newark to Brant Broughton (Travel Wright).

Parking: The inn has a large car park, which you may use while you undertake the walk.

Length of the walk: 4$^{1}/_{2}$ miles. (It is possible to reduce this to 3$^{3}/_{4}$ miles, by taking a short cut, but this could present some slight difficulty.) Maps: OS Landranger 121 Lincoln, Pathfinder 797 Newark-on-Trent East (inn GR 858525).

Barnby in the Willows is an attractive village, right on the Lincolnshire county boundary. As often happens in such cases, the most appealing routes straddle the boundary. On this walk, we leave Nottinghamshire almost immediately after setting out, and go over fertile arable and grass fields to reach the charming Lincolnshire village of Beckingham. From here, a scenic riverside stroll along the Nottinghamshire bank of the Witham brings us back to Barnby.

The Walk

Follow Front Street through the village. Look out as you go for Barnby's circular medieval dovecote – the smallest of three in Nottinghamshire. This is set back from the road and it does not appear to be accessible to the public.

48

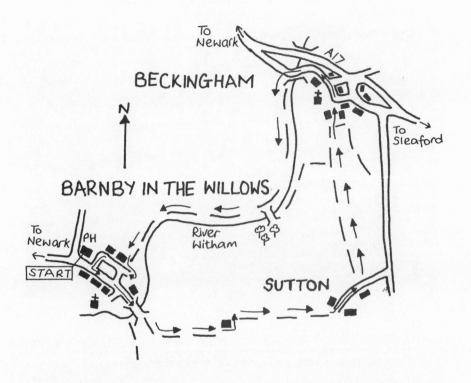

On reaching a right-hand bend, just before the church, keep straight ahead along the drive of Barnby Hall. Although this is labelled as a private drive, there is clear evidence of pedestrian access, along the drive only, to the farm track beyond. Cross the river Witham, keeping to the farm track and swinging left with it, beside a small wood, and passing a collection of farm buildings. At the end of the buildings, turn left, then right again, still following the clearly defined track. Ignore a newer farm track on its right. Reach a wooded lane, and continue ahead to reach the hamlet of Sutton.

After passing, on your left, Fairview Stud, and just before Apricot Hall (on the right), turn left over a stile, following the waymarked public footpath. This proves to be a somewhat interesting footpath, in that the condition of the stiles and waymarks appears to depend on the whim of the individual occupiers. Several hedges have been removed, too, which has resulted in a preponderence of L-shaped fields.

The River Witham.

Follow the hedge partway over the first field, until it bends sharp left. Continue ahead here, bearing very slightly right, to reach a gap in the fence and hedge. From here the path continues more or less straight ahead, all the way to Beckingham. At the angle of the second L-shaped field, cross a dilapidated stile and continue on the left of the hedge until you reach a small enclosure (no stile) beside a trough and, just beyond, a stile leading into the next field, now on the right of the hedge.

Partway down this field, a stile on the left offers the opportunity for a short cut. Over the stile, a waymarked path leads down the right of the field. The Pathfinder map indicates it as swinging left over the next field to reach the eastern bank of the Witham. When I came, this field had a growing crop and the exit onto the riverside was over a fence, topped with barbed wire. The final section, from here to the bridge by Skerries Plantation, is no problem. But this short cut should be regarded as a suggestion only, without any recommendation!

Keeping to the main route, continue to the right of the hedge and fence over this and the next field, turning right at the end to cross the top of the field, passing a farm gate. Cross a stile and turn left immediately over a second stile, continuing through to the road in Beckingham village.

Turn left at a road junction and then right. Go left near the church to cross the river by the Black Swan restaurant. Arrive back in Nottinghamshire.

Turn left over the bridge, following the riverside path. The flood bank is a better bet than the lower path on this first section, being less closed in, and with fewer nettles.

Beyond Skerries Plantation, the flood bank fades out, but a good path continues all the way to the outskirts of Barnby. Watch the waymarks (yellow arrows on posts) carefully. For the most part these point the way straight ahead along the riverside. When level with the village, an arrow will be seen to point away from the river, in the direction of the houses. Follow this over the field to reach an angle in the hedge. Turn right here, following another arrow along the hedge-side. At the next arrow turn left, passing a stile (with no fence!) and follow an enclosed green path to Back Lane.

Turn right and follow Back Lane and Cross Lane to reach Front Street, turning right again here, back to the inn.

Places of interest nearby

At nearby Newark-on-Trent can be found *Newark Castle*, open daily throughout the year; *Millgate Folk Museum* also open daily but telephone 01636 79403 to confirm exact times; and *Newark Air Museum*, located at Winthorpe, just north of Newark, again open daily.

11 Fiskerton
The Bromley Arms

This attractive 17th century inn stands on the wharf in the pleasant riverside village of Fiskerton. It was traditionally used by the bargemen on the river and at one time included stabling for the horses. A popular venue for people boating, walkers and day-trippers, the Bromley is described by the landlord as 'The pub on the river, offering good food, good ales, and good company', a sentiment with which we would not disagree.

A Hardys and Hansons inn, the Bromley is open from 11.30 am until 2.30 pm and 6 pm until 11 pm, Monday to Saturday (7 pm until 11 pm in winter). Sunday opening is from 12 noon until 3 pm and 7 pm until 10.30 pm. The speciality ales are Kimberley Best and Classic. Food is obtainable, both meals and snacks, every lunchtime, and in the evenings from Tuesday to Saturday. Specialities include Bromley braised steak and onions with Guinness gravy. There are daily specials as well, and the traditional three-course Sunday lunch. The gi-normous sausage cobs are highly recommended. Children are specially catered for, with such mouth-watering delights as

fishysaurus, chicken teddies and the always popular bangers 'n' beans. It goes without saying that families are welcome here, although there is no special room set apart for them. There is a non-smoking section, and dogs may come too, if well-behaved.
Telephone: 01636 830789.

How to get there: From Southwell, follow Church Street past the Minster and the public car park, turning right at the end to follow the unclassified road signposted for Fiskerton. Turn right in the village, at the T-junction, and you will find the Bromley Arms a little way along on your left.

Parking: The landlord does not mind if you leave your car here for an hour or two while you walk (if you are a customer, of course). There is alternative parking on the Rolleston road.

Length of the walk: 2¹/₂ miles. Maps: OS Landranger 120 Mansfield and the Dukeries, Pathfinder 796 Newark-on-Trent West (inn GR 737511).

This pleasant short walk begins at Fiskerton Wharf, itself a place of some interest, with its ancient buildings and its rivercraft. The route passes the 18th century Fiskerton Mill and visits the neighbouring village of Rolleston.

The Walk
Follow the wharf-top path downstream. The outer rim of the wharf is vertical and there is no guard-rail, so keep your children on a tight lead for this short distance. On reaching the road and the public car park, cross over and enter the field directly opposite. There are two guide-posts here, the right-hand one being relevant for our purpose. This points diagonally over the field, although this does not appear to be strictly accurate. Our observations, with a growing crop in the field, were that the path crosses from a point directly opposite the nearside end of a pair of cottages, a little way into the field. An alternative follows the top of the flood bank around from just inside the gateway, to reach the same point.

Cross the flood bank and continue over a dyke, then over the river Greet, passing ancient Fiskerton Mill. The mill, built about 1760, was originally a lace-thread factory, but was later converted into a corn

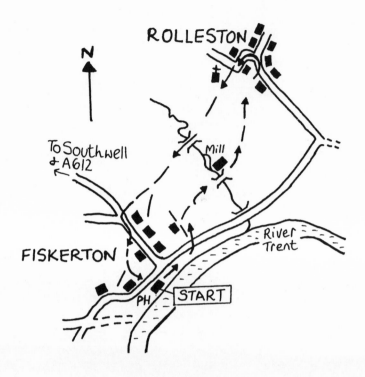

mill. It is rather a sad-looking building today, no longer, it seems, in use as a mill, and not open to the public.

Turning left around the side of the building, cross a stile on your right and follow the edge of the ensuing field. Pass through a wooded area before crossing a footbridge and bearing left along a delightful tree-lined path. Continue on beside the next open field, walking directly towards the church tower at Rolleston.

The OS map shows the path as continuing over the next large field in more or less the same direction, but bearing a little to the right. You may find that it has been diverted a bit and, if this is the case, follow the diversion markers. The regular line is rejoined in the angle of the hedge towards the far side of the field, and to the right of the church. You will see 'Trent Valley Way' markers here, pointing the way along the left of the hedge away from you.

Follow the hedge for a little way before turning right to reach a gate by a barn conversion development. Turn left here and follow an enclosed path to the road.

Fiskerton Wharf.

Turn left through Rolleston village, bearing left again at a second bend where a welcome seat offers an excellent opportunity for a brief rest before continuing along the side road to reach the church gate. Enter the gate and follow the church pathway to meet the angle of the church wall. Bear left here between the graves to reach and cross a stile in the corner of the churchyard.

Keep straight ahead over the field, turning right a little on reaching the far side to reach and cross another stile. Walk on again, crossing the river Greet and the Beck Dyke by two sturdy wooden footbridges. From here follow a clear field-side track, on the right of the hedge, to join the road just outside Fiskerton, and turn left.

Beside the Stable Salon turn right, following the waymarked path. In a housing estate, turn left at the road junction/turning point. On reaching a branch in the path take the kissing-gate on the left. Cross a field to reach the road – and journey's end.

Places of interest nearby
Take time out to visit *Southwell Minster*, just to the north-west of Fiskerton.

55

East Stoke
The Pauncefote Arms

The tiny village of East Stoke has interest out of all proportion to its size: it bestrides the Roman Fosse Way, a major battle of the Wars of the Roses was fought here and the inn bears the name of the first British Ambassador to the United States, Lord Pauncefote. His home was at Stoke Hall and his tomb is in the churchyard nearby. The final bloody battle of the Wars of the Roses took place at East Stoke, reputedly around the site of the inn, which itself dates from about 1700. It is altogether more peaceful hereabouts today, the only interruption in the tranquillity being occasioned by the passage of traffic on the busy Roman road.

This friendly village pub with its courteous and helpful licensees and staff is unusual in that, although it is not a freehouse, neither is it tied to any one of the big breweries, but belongs instead to the Centric Pub Co. plc. You can get Stones Bitter here and also Theakston ales, and the speciality draught cider is Scrumpy Jack. The lunchtime opening hours are 12 noon to 3 pm from Sunday to Friday and, in the evenings, 5.30 pm to 11 pm from Monday to

Friday, and 7 pm to 10.30 pm on Sunday. On Saturday, the pub is open all day, from 11 am through to 11 pm. Meals and bar snacks are available during normal opening hours, and a take-away service is also provided. The menu is displayed on a board in the lounge bar and may include, for example, steak and ale pie, pork spare ribs, chicken curry and jacket potatoes. And, for afters, how about the deep dish apple or cherry pie? Alternatively, you can settle for a ploughman's lunch, or a salad. If a sandwich is all you require, we can recommend the delicious 'Scufflers'. Families are welcome here and, although there is no specific family room, there is a children's play area as well as a non-smoking section. Well-behaved dogs are welcome, too.

Telephone: 01636 525226.

How to get there: It couldn't be easier! Just follow the A46 (Fosse Way), southwards from Newark (4 miles), or from Saxondale, if you are coming from Nottingham or the south. The Pauncefote Arms is an unmistakable building on the east side of the Fosse, at the village crossroads.

East Stoke is on the Nottingham to Newark bus routes operated by Road Car and Pathfinder.

Parking: You may leave your vehicle in the pub car park while you ramble – but it is polite to ask.

Length of the walk: 4³/₄ miles. Maps: OS Landranger 129 Nottingham and Loughborough, Pathfinder 813 Carlton and Elston (inn GR 754496).

This walk is in two halves, separated by the busy Fosse Way – you will need to cross the Roman road twice. In the first stage of the walk we go by quiet paths down to the riverside, passing on the way the now peaceful site of the climax to that awful battle of some 500 years ago. Crossing over to the east of the road, we visit the pretty village of Elston, once the home of a famous family.

The Walk

Cross carefully over the Fosse Way and follow School Lane. Immediately after passing under a brick-built bridge (connecting the parts of Stoke Hall grounds) you come to the church entrance, on

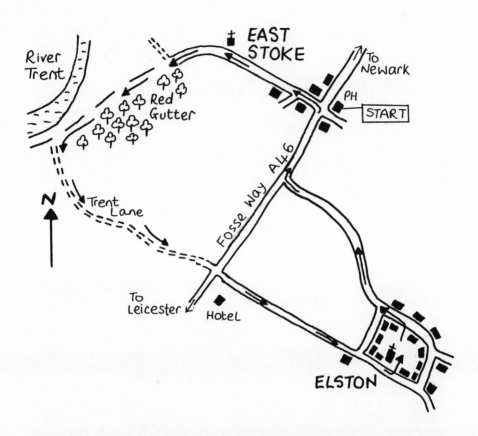

your right. The grave of Lord Pauncefote is here in the churchyard, guarded by a splendid bronze angel. Although little appears to be generally known today of the former ambassador, it is understood that, during his term of office, believed to have been from 1889 to 1902, he was instrumental in improving considerably the relations between Britain and America, and in healing a serious rift which had developed between the two nations.

From the church, continue round to the left with the road, passing the hall entrance. On reaching a right-hand bend, leave the road and cross a large hard-standing, continuing on along a footpath beside Stoke Wood. At the top of the rise, bear right a little from the wood, keeping to the grassy pathway.

At this point, where the path deviates from the wood, you pass Red Gutter – the climactic point of the battle of Stoke Field. The

58

The archway at East Stoke.

battle is thought to have been fought around the area of the modern crossroads, and the Yorkist rebels were driven down towards the river, passing through the trench now known as Red Gutter, so named from the blood that flowed there. In the course of the conflict, many thousands of men are said to have died.

If you stand on the edge of the wood here – you may not enter – you will be able to identify the hollow of Red Gutter, now overgrown and unmarked.

Continue along the grassy path. Opposite the end of the woods, cross a field beside the river and turn left into a rough trackway – Trent Lane. Ascend the hill, pausing partway, by a tall tree, to enjoy the grand views over the Trent valley, including the lock and weir at Hazelford, and the river traffic.

The track levels out, and there are now fine, wide views ahead, over the Vale of Belvoir, to Belvoir Castle itself on its wooded hilltop. Pass through a handgate beside a farm gate and reach the Fosse Way. Cross over, again with care, and follow the road ahead to Elston.

A seat by the roadside as you approach Elston, though a little low, offers a welcome opportunity for a rest. The inscription on the back, badly weathered now, is intriguing. We were unable to read all of it, but gathered that it had been provided in recognition of 'The Winner(s) of the Maths Scrapbook Competition'!

Pass Elston Hall on your right. This was the family home of the Darwin family from the 17th century. Erasmus Darwin, the scientist and grandfather of Charles Darwin, was born at Elston.

Pass Pinfold Lane, too, opposite the hall, on your left, following Top Street. Turn left by the church – waymarked to the village hall – and follow a footway past the Old School House, a modern school and a playing field. Continue along a delightful footpath to Low Street and turn left.

After passing Pinfold Lane again, carry on along the lane all the way to its end. A footpath marked on the map partway along the lane, and suggesting a short cut, appears to have been extinguished, so the road is Hobson's choice. Turn right and follow the Fosse Way (thankfully, there is a footpath here) back to the inn.

13 Brinsley
The Yew Tree

The Yew Tree is an attractive, traditional, oak-beamed village inn, smart but not flashy, with accommodation consisting of a single, spacious bar-cum-lounge and incorporating an integral dining area. Special facilities are somewhat limited and there is no separate family room or play area. But families are welcome, nonetheless, and there are picnic tables at the front.

A Hardys and Hansons house, the hours of opening are from 11.30 am to 2.30 pm and 5.30 pm to 11 pm, Monday to Saturday, and 12 noon to 3 pm and 7 pm to 10.30 pm on Sunday. The speciality ales include Kimberley Classic, Best Bitter and Mild. The cider is Dry Blackthorn, and the lagers are Heineken and Tennent's. There is a comprehensive list of wines. Food is available on weekdays from 12 noon to 2 pm and 6.30 pm to 8.30 pm, and on Sundays from 11.45 am to 2 pm and 6.45 pm to 8.30 pm. A full range of meals and bar snacks is on offer, from basic sandwiches to succulent steaks, seafood and shellfish. You can enjoy chicken curry, a weekly speciality pie, roast of the day, or fresh fish on Thursdays, not to

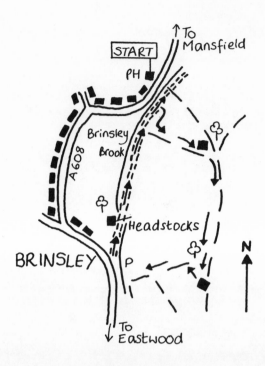

mention the traditional Sunday lunch. Vegetarian dishes are always available.

Telephone: 01773 715881.

How to get there: Follow the A608 Eastwood to Mansfield road (accessed either from junction 27 of the M1 or the A610 Kimberley bypass). The inn is on the west side of the road at the northern end of Brinsley.

The village is served by Trent buses between Nottingham and Alfreton.

Parking: You may leave your car for a while in the inn car park. Alternatively, there is a public car park at the Brinsley picnic area, about 1 mile south of here, by which the walk passes.

Length of the walk: 2½ miles. Maps: OS Landranger 129 Nottingham and Loughborough, Pathfinder 812 Nottingham North and Ilkeston (inn GR 469498).

The Brinsley headstocks.

Brinsley is in the heart of D.H. Lawrence country. The author's father worked in the pit here, and our route takes us first along quiet ways known and loved by D.H. himself. We visit, too, the site of Brinsley Colliery. The colliery itself has ceased to exist, but the headstocks have been re-erected on the site, to serve as a reminder, not just of Lawrence, but also of the hardships endured in the past by those, some of them mere children, who once toiled beneath these green fields. The surrounding area has been landscaped to form a delightful picnic area. We return via the former colliery railway track, now reverted to a pleasant country footpath.

The Walk

Cross the road and follow the waymarked footpath, passing to the left of a modern bungalow to reach the track of the former Brinsley railway line. Turn right onto the track and follow this lovely rural path until you reach a farm area on your right. Descend by steps to reach a stile on the left of the track and cross over into the adjacent field.

Bear left over the field, making for a stile in the far left-hand corner, beneath a power line. Cross the stile, between a pair of farm

63

gates, and follow the fence on your left.

Pass to the right of Willey Wood Farm, crossing two more stiles beside farm gates, then turn right to cross the next field diagonally on a clear, broad track, continuing then beside the fence over a second long field. There are splendid wide views from here over the Derbyshire borderlands.

On reaching a handgate, pass through and bear left around the side of the field to reach a gate leading into Coneygrey Farm. Do not go through the gate, however, but turn right and follow the hedge on your left to reach another gate and stile, to the left of Coneygrey Plantation. Cross the stile and turn left, again following the field boundary.

After passing a stile on your left, bear right, making for a large, unprepossessing red-brick building. Cross a stile at its right-hand end and follow the metalled path to the road. Turn right.

Follow the road for a very short distance to reach the picnic site car park, giving access to the former railway, which is now followed all the way back to the starting point of the walk. A short diversion, however, a little way along the track on the left, will bring you to the picnic site itself, and the Brinsley Headstocks – an impressive reminder of the little township's past.

Places of interest nearby
To the south of Brinsley, at 8a Victoria Street, Eastwood, is the *D.H. Lawrence Birthplace Museum*. It is open daily throughout the year except over the Christmas and New Year period.

14 Lambley
The Nag's Head

The Nag's Head, formerly a farmhouse, was built in the 18th century. A typical old-style village inn, the low beams and half-timbered interior effect, together with the open fire and horse-brasses, accentuate the genuine charm of this popular house.

The inn belongs to Scottish and Newcastle, and the ales on offer include Home Bitter and Mild, Theakston XB and Best Bitter and Marston's Pedigree. Scrumpy Jack cider is on draught, and McEwan's lager is also found here. The pub is open daily, except Sunday, from 11 am to 3 pm and 5 pm to 11 pm. Sunday hours are from 12 noon to 3 pm and 7 pm to 10.30 pm. Meals and bar snacks are available daily, from Monday to Saturday, between 12 noon and 2 pm. Evening catering is from 6 pm until 8 pm on Tuesdays, and between 6 pm and 8.45 pm from Wednesday to Saturday. No meals are provided on Sunday, or on Monday evening. The customer is spoilt for choice at the 'Nag's', where the menu offers an impressive range of full meals and snacks, all at reasonable prices. Curries, salads, jacket potatoes, giant filled Yorkshire puddings, ploughman's lunches, sandwiches and snacks, all these, and others, are here. In addition, there are 'daily specials' posted up on the bar blackboard. Some vegetarian dishes are also served. Families can relax here, and there is both a family room and a children's play area. There is a beer garden, too, and dogs are welcome if well-behaved. On those days when food is not available, the licensees do not object to patrons eating their own food in the outside drinking area.

Telephone: 0115 9312546.

How to get there: From the B684 Nottingham to Woodborough road, turn east at Mapperley Plains, following either Catfoot Lane or Spring Lane, to reach Lambley. The Nag's Head is at the western end of the village.

Lambley is served by Barton's Nottingham to Calverton buses.

Parking: Customers may leave their wheels in the pub car park for an hour or two, while they walk. There are also a few roadside spaces.

Length of the walk: Route A 2½ miles. *Route B* 2¼ miles. Maps: OS Landranger 129 Nottingham and Loughborough, Pathfinder 813 Carlton and Elston (inn GR 628452).

Lambley is famous for its dumbles, a dumble being the local name for a shallow dale with a stream. We offer a choice of two short strolls here, both of which take the walker along the course of one or other of the dumbles. The second route also offers the opportunity to visit the excellent Floralands Garden Centre and, for the kiddies' benefit, Playworld.

The Walk
Route A
Set out from the inn, following Spring Lane (right, along the main road). Turn right again immediately to follow the waymarked footpath – a pretty woodland path, with the deep ravine of Lambley Dumble on your right. Emerge into a field and continue ahead, to re-enter the wooded area, still keeping to the left of the dumble.

On reaching a footbridge, resist the impulse to cross, bearing left instead to follow the hedge on your right for a little way, before swinging left over the field to reach a stile and a gap in the hedge. Cross a green track and follow the clear path straight ahead over

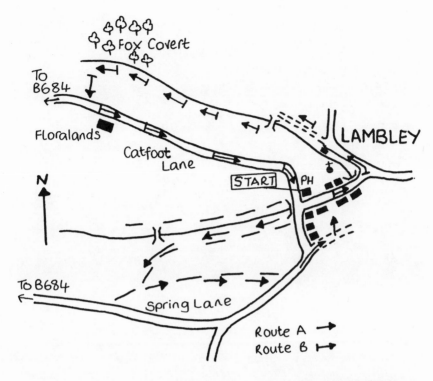

two fields (one big, one small). At the end of the second field turn sharp left into an enclosed lane. Take care, because the way may be overgrown and uneven underfoot.

Pass a farm entrance, and the Hillview Stables, still keeping to the enclosed way for a short distance. Enter a field, with wide views over Lambley. Follow the right-hand side of two fields, bearing left in the third and making for a group of houses.

At the road, cross over and follow the waymarked track to the right of the houses. Just before a farm gate, turn left over a plank bridge and follow a fenced path through to an access road and Main Street. Turn left for the inn.

Route B
Turn left from the pub and follow Main Street past Lambley Spring, before turning left onto the Woodborough road. When the road bends right by the Woodlarks Inn, keep straight ahead, following an unmade road (The Dumbles) on the right of a stream.

A corner of Floralands Garden Centre.

Where a path crosses from right to left, turn left to cross the stream by a footbridge, doubling back to the right on reaching the fields to follow the hedge-side over a series of fields. This is a beautiful field path with excellent stiles.

At the end of Fox Covert, turn left at the guide post, following the hedge-side to the road (Catfoot Lane). Turn left for Floralands and Playworld.

From Floralands, follow the road back to Lambley, enjoying the excellent views ahead and to your left. But take care here. There is no pavement, so keep well in to the right-hand side of the road.

Places of interest nearby

At Calverton, just to the north of Lambley, can be found the *Calverton Framework Knitters' Cottages*. In Main Street, Calverton, is a *folk museum* which is open by prior arrangement (telephone 0115 9652836).

15 Strelley
The Broad Oak

The Broad Oak is a charming inn in a rural setting, in complete contradiction of its situation just a few hundred yards from one of the biggest council estates in the city of Nottingham. This 300 year old hostelry has been completely refurbished, yet still retains the character of a typical old-world village inn. Set back from the road, amid many mature trees (including, appropriately enough, a broad oak), the inn is popular with locals and with visitors from further afield.

A Hardys and Hansons house, the ales include Kimberley Mild, Bitter and Classic. The ciderholic can choose from Strongbow, Woodpecker and Scrumpy Jack, and the lager drinker from Heineken and Stella. There is also a wide selection of red, white and house wines, sparkling wines, champagne and non-alcoholic beverages. The Broad Oak is open all day, from 11 am to 11 pm in the week (Monday to Saturday) and from 12 noon to 10.30 pm on Sunday. Bar snacks and full meals are available every day, from opening time through to 9 pm and an impressive menu offers satisfaction to all tastes. If a light snack is all you want, you can settle for a delicious sandwich or salad, a 4 oz beefburger (with or without cheese) or a giant jacket potato with the filling of your choice. Main courses include pork steak and rump steak, grilled lamb chops, fisherman's pie, liver and onions and curry. Then there are the daily specials, posted up on the blackboard, and the traditional Sunday roast. Families are welcome here and, while there is no specific family room, there is a children's play area. The youngsters have their own menu – as also, incidentally, do vegetarians. There is a delightful beer garden, and dogs are welcome outside, though not in the kiddies' area.

Telephone: 0115 9293340.

How to get there: From the outer ring road on the west side of Nottingham, follow Aspley Lane and Strelley Road through to the junction (marked by traffic lights) with the A6002 Nuthall/Stapleford/M1 link road. Cross over and follow Main Street. The Broad Oak is about 100 yards along on the right.

Nottingham Corporation operate bus services along both Strelley Road and the A6002, to within 100 yards of the inn.

Parking: The Broad Oak has its own car park, where customers are welcome to leave their vehicles for the duration of their walk. But it is worth mentioning that a little over 1 mile of road walking can be lopped off the walk if you start from just beyond the village church, where limited roadside parking is possible.

Length of the walk: 4³/₄ miles (or 3¹/₂ miles if starting and finishing beyond the church, and 5³/₄ miles if including the optional extension around Oldmoor Wood). Maps: OS Landranger 129 Nottingham and Loughborough, Pathfinder 812 Nottingham North and Ilkeston (inn GR 513419).

Despite the close proximity of the city of Nottingham and the M1 motorway, and a long tradition of coal mining (the first recorded mines in the county were in this area, in the 13th century), the Strelley district remains surprisingly rural and unspoilt. In the course of this walk a memorial to three local men who fought at Waterloo is visited. This is shoulder to shoulder with a similar memorial to those who died in more recent wars. An optional extension offers a stroll around a pleasant woodland reserve.

70

The Waterloo Memorial at Cossall.

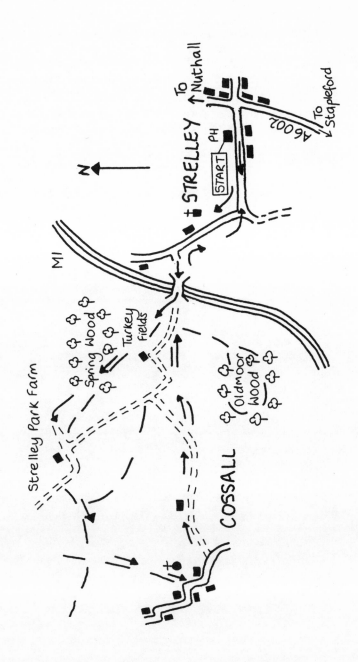

The Walk

Follow the main street from the inn, passing the church, until you reach a wayside seat beside a waymarked track on the left. Leave the road and follow the track over the motorway bridge, taking a footpath on the right, waymarked for Awsworth and Cossall. Follow the field's edge, with a wood on your left, continuing ahead over two fields and passing by Turkey Fields Farm (all the turkeys in the field when we came were geese!) to reach a stile leading into Spring Wood.

Follow a meandering path through the wood, cross one field, and then follow the fence up the left of a second, to reach a lane and turn left.

Pass Strelley Park Farm and keep straight on over the cross-ways, swinging right with the lane to reach a footpath, waymarked for Cossall village, on your left. Cross the stile and follow the hedge. At the end of the third field turn left, by another 'Cossall village' guide-post, making for the spire of Cossall church, visible now on the hilltop ahead. Keep on over the fields to reach an access lane and the village street, turning left to reach the church.

Pause a while here to visit the memorial to the local heroes of Waterloo. There clearly are still people hereabouts who care, for there were fresh flowers on the memorial when we came.

Leaving the church, continue around the bend of the road, keeping straight ahead at the next junction and following Robinettes Lane. Pass an industrial estate and leave the road on the next bend to follow the waymarked path for Strelley. Cross this big field, corner to corner, passing to the left of a distant oak tree. Go over the stile in the corner of the field and follow the hedge and the ensuing lane.

When the lane bends to the left, leave by a footpath on the right, following this and the succeeding lane back to the motorway bridge and Strelley.

Before returning to Strelley, you are recommended to turn off right, just before the motorway, to visit Oldmoor Wood, a property of the Woodland Trust. Visitors are welcome here, but please keep to the marked paths.

Places of interest nearby

South-east of Strelley is *Wollaton Hall* which is open daily except Christmas Day. A *natural history museum* is also housed here.

16 Stoke Bardolph
The Ferry Boat

The Ferry Boat is an inn full of character. Dating back over 150 years, it takes its name from the ferry which used to ply between here and Shelford, across the Trent. A notice beside the door tells us that the inn is flooded on average once every three years. No insurance company is prepared to accept the risk, so the proprietors are obliged to bear the cost of the inevitable heavy damage. They continue to do so – 'because we love the place'. The inn has seen many changes, and has been tastefully refurbished. The accommodation has been extended by taking in various stables and barns in order to retain the traditional warm and friendly atmosphere. Revolutionary facilities have been introduced, including a children's indoor soft play room, disabled loos and ramps, braille menus and a heated courtyard. There is both a beer garden and a non-smoking section – and you may bring the dog, provided you keep him/her on the front lawn or in the courtyard. The spacious dining area is a pleasing blend of old and new, where the up-to-date decor does not clash with the traditional appearance of the low ceilings and old timbers.

The Ferry Boat belongs to Greenalls Premier House Group, and the range of ales includes Greenalls Original, Shipstone's and Tetley. Strongbow cider is here, on draught, and the lagers are Carling, Labatt's and Tennent's. There is a range of wines which embraces the house dry, medium and red, French Campanard, Liebfraumilch and Eisberg. The inn is open all day, 11 am to 11 pm, from Monday to Saturday. On Sundays the licensing hours are 12 noon to 3 pm and 7 pm to 10.30 pm although the pub is open all day for food. Meals and bar snacks are available every day, both at lunchtime and in the evening. On Sundays you can get food at any time between 12 noon and 9.30 pm. The rest of the week there is a break from 2.30 pm to 5 pm, but the evening session is extended, on Friday and Saturday, to 10 pm.

The menu is so comprehensive that recommending specialities is well-nigh impossible. But how about farmhouse chicken pie, haddock and cauliflower cheese, beef suet pudding, or honey baked ham platter? There is a mouth-watering selection of sweets and sundaes to follow, and a full range of sandwiches for those of lighter appetite. If you fancy a traditional Sunday lunch, you will get that here, too. Neither are the children forgotten, nor those of mature years, nor vegetarians. There is something for everyone down at the Ferry Boat inn.

Telephone: 0115 9871232.

How to get there: From the A612 Nottingham to Southwell road, turn off right just after passing under the railway bridge at Gedling. If coming from the Southwell direction, turn off left, 1 mile past Burton Joyce. The turning is signposted for Stoke Bardolph. Follow the road through the village and the Ferry Boat will be found directly on the riverside.

Parking: It is all right to leave your car here while following your walk, but it is not really necessary, as there is ample parking available in the riverside public car park.

Length of the walk: 4^1/$_2$ miles. Maps: OS Landranger 129 Nottingham and Loughborough, Pathfinder 813 Carlton and Elston (inn GR 647421).

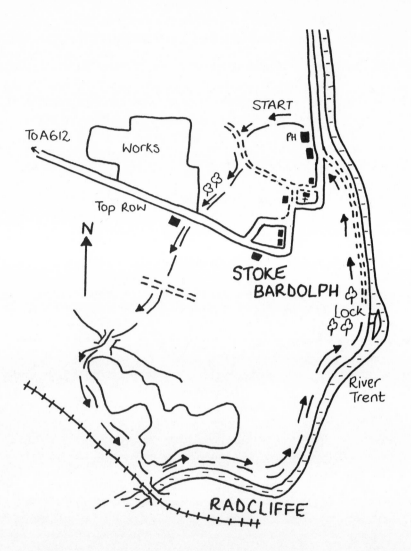

The little village of Stoke Bardolph is tucked away at the end of a quiet side road, hidden from the busy Nottingham to Southwell road, and it is easy to forget how close you are to the rush and bustle of the city. The riverside here is particularly popular, with its swans and its boats. Our route takes us first over quiet field paths, passing close by former colliery lagoons, before returning along the riverbank, where we visit the picturesque Stoke Lock.

The Walk

Caution: the first stage of the walk passes close to a deep and fast-flowing stream, and it might be wise to omit this section if you have adventurous children (or adventurous dogs), and follow the road as far as the Top Row cottages (by the 'No Speed Limit' sign).

Pass by the inn, and the popular children's play area, and cross a stile on your left. Bear right through a copse and turn left to follow the side of a stream. This is the outflow from the Severn-Trent treatment works and, as mentioned above, is very deep and fast-flowing. On reaching the top end of the embankment, turn left to follow a metalled lane. Where the lane swings sharply left, bear right a little to follow a green track, with a hedge on your left. Continue along a footpath beside a wood to reach the road by Top Row cottages, and cross over.

Follow the hedge over three long fields, crossing a farm lane after the second field, to reach and cross a footbridge over the Ouse Dyke. Follow a track round to the right, then left again, with a hedge on your left and a trading estate away to the right. Keep an embankment on your left until you reach a barrier gate.

Passing through Stoke Lock.

From here you have a choice of routes. You may pass round the left of the gate and continue along the same track until you reach the riverside. Or you might prefer to ascend the steep bank on your left and follow a higher-level path beside the colliery lagoons – the outlook is better here than on the enclosed lower path. Descend again when you reach the river.

Turn left along the riverside path, with a good view here across the river to Radcliffe on Trent church, and the many-arched railway viaduct.

The riverside path is very overgrown at first, but improves all the time, and is a pleasant walk throughout. The high point is Stoke Lock. This is less well known than Gunthorpe Lock, a few miles downstream, but just as attractive, and an excellent point at which to pause for a few minutes and watch the river traffic.

The obvious way back to Stoke will take you along the metalled access road, but a worthwhile alternative follows a vestigial footpath, closer by the waterside.

Places of interest nearby
Colwick Country Park, south-west of Stoke Bardolph, is well worth a visit.

17 Car Colston
The Royal Oak

The Royal Oak is a welcoming family inn overlooking the green at the southern end of Car Colston village. Approximately 200 years old, the building was once a hosiery factory. An interesting feature of the house is the unusual arched brick ceilings in the lounge and in the cellar. Another feature of the cellar, we are told, is the ghost of a Roman centurion – Car Colston is close to the Fosse Way, and not far from the Roman station of Margidunum. Only the top half of the spectre is seen, apparently, because the earth level has changed in 2,000 years. On a more up-to-date note, the lounge features an interesting collection of copperware, and a number of excellent pictures – which may be purchased – by Jon Nicholls, a local artist. The bar-room has a collection of old nameplates, house and road signs and so on, fixed to the front of the counter, and old brass barrel-taps tucked under the oak beams.

The daily opening hours are from 12 noon to 3 pm and 6.30 pm to 11 pm (7 pm to 10.30 pm on Sunday evenings). The house belongs to Mansfield Brewery and the speciality ale is Old Baily.

Bottled cider is available, both sweet and dry. Grolsch and Foster's lagers are sold here, and French house wines. Meals and bar snacks are served daily at lunchtime and every evening except Sunday and Monday. You may dine on deep fried chicken, a succulent sirloin steak, home-made lasagne or chicken Kiev. Or a tasty ploughman's. The choice of snacks includes mushrooms in crispy batter, jacket potatoes, burgers, salads and sandwiches, and daily specials are displayed on the blackboard at the bar. There is no play area, but families are welcome. There is a family room as well as a beer garden, and the fact that the inn is on the green is a plus. Well-behaved dogs are welcome, too. It is also possible to camp here.

Telephone: 01949 20247.

How to get there: Car Colston lies just to the east of the A46 (Fosse Way), south-west of Newark. Leave the Roman road by an unclassified minor road, signposted for Car Colston and Screveton, 1 mile north-east of the Newton roundabout. Car Colston is reached after about ¹/₂ mile, and the Royal Oak will be seen directly ahead of you, on the far side of the green.

Car Colston is served by the Road Car bus service between Newark and Bingham.

Parking: You may leave your car here while undertaking the walk.

Length of the walk: 3¹/₂ miles. Maps: OS Landranger 129 Nottingham and Loughborough, Pathfinder 813 Carlton and Elston (inn GR 719426).

The charming village of Car Colston is unique in possessing not one, but two greens; one at each end of the village. Our route follows the village street from one to the other, passing close by the former home of Robert Thoroton, our county's most celebrated antiquarian. We visit the neighbouring village of Scarrington; a place which has its own special interest – or should we say, curiosity? Then back to Car Colston by quiet and pleasant field paths.

The Walk

Cross the road from the inn and follow the Screveton road through the village and past the parish church. After negotiating a double bend

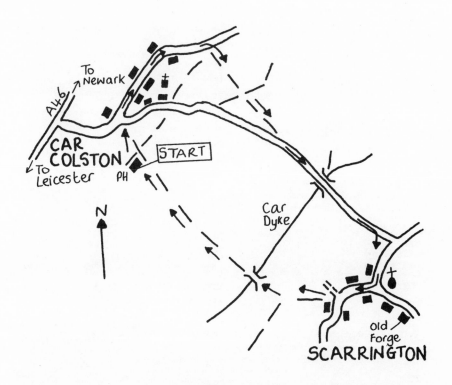

by the Old Hall, reach the little green. There are two guide-posts here, one indicating a footpath and the other a bridleway. Take the bridleway route, crossing the green diagonally to reach a farm gate. Pass through, and follow the hedge on your left over two fields, crossing a ditch and bearing left to reach a road, Car Lane.

Keep straight forward along the lane. There is no footway here, so keep well in to the right. At the top of the rise, after going under a power line, pass one field and then take a waymarked footpath on the right, crossing this field diagonally and heading to the left of the church spire, to reach Scarrington. Turn right and follow the village street.

At the bend by the church, deviate left along the Aslockton road to reach the Old Forge – and Scarrington's little curiosity, a 17 ft stack of discarded horseshoes, about 50,000 in number, which the local blacksmith constructed between 1945 and 1965.

Retrace your steps to the church and bear left, following the main street through the village. At the Methodist chapel, turn right

The pile of horseshoes at Scarrington.

and, almost immediately, left onto a waymarked footpath directly opposite a barn conversion development. Cross the field diagonally and, in the far corner, pass through the hedge and turn half-right to continue down the field. At the end of this field bear left, to cross the Car Dyke by a footbridge, before continuing on the same line as before, with the hedge on your right, until you reach a pair of farm gates.

Cross the adjacent stile (this one has a doggie-flap as well!) and keep straight on down the field, following the clear farm track back to the big green.

Places of interest nearby
West of Car Colston, situated on the river Trent, is the village of *Gunthorpe*, with its lock and riverside walks.

18 Cropwell Butler
The Plough

Parts of the Plough, a pleasant and friendly traditional village inn, date from the 18th century, and the low beamed ceilings and real coal fires, on cold days, emphasise the welcoming atmosphere. The landlady prides herself on the quality of her cuisine, the speciality here being good, home-cooked food, prepared to order from fresh local produce. This house is one of Scottish and Newcastle's (Home Brewery), and the various ales on sale include both Home ales and Theakston.

Opening hours are from 11.30 am to 2.30 pm, Monday to Friday, 11.30 am to 3 pm on Saturday and 12 noon to 3 pm on Sunday. The pub is open in the evening from 6 pm to 11 pm on Monday to Friday, 6.30 pm to 11 pm on Saturday and 7 pm to 10.30 pm on Sunday. Snacks and lunches are available daily from 12.15 pm to 2 pm, with evening dinner from 7 pm to 9 pm on Monday to Wednesday and 7 pm to 10 pm on Thursday to Saturday. A full menu includes a selection of starters and main courses, among which seafood, pasta, chicken and steak dishes figure prominently. You can complete your meal with a choice of various sweets, followed with liqueur (or straight) coffee. The light bites on offer include an appetising selection of sandwiches. A traditional Sunday lunch is also provided here. There is no separate family room or children's play area at the Plough, but families are welcome. There is a beer garden, and dogs are also permitted, but not inside, please.

Telephone: 0115 9333124.

How to get there: From the A52 Nottingham to Grantham road, turn off at the Cropwell road junction on the Radcliffe on Trent bypass (traffic lights). Follow the road up the hill away from Radcliffe and over the A46 Fosse Way. Continue into Cropwell Butler village as the road bends rightward, and the Plough will be found on the right.

Parking: You are welcome to leave your car here while you take your walk.

Length of the walk: 2½ miles (3½ miles if you include the optional extension). Maps: OS Landranger 129 Nottingham and Loughborough, Pathfinder 834 Radcliffe on Trent (inn GR 685370).

There are two Cropwells, Cropwell Bishop, 1 mile south of Cropwell Butler, being the larger of the two. This short circular walk takes us over the fields to follow the towpath of the former Grantham Canal, returning via pleasant Hoe Hill Wood. The optional extension continues through to Cropwell Bishop, but omits Hoe Hill.

The Walk

Leaving the inn, turn right along Main Street, then right again to follow a narrow passageway – The Posts – through to Back Lane. Turn right again and follow the lane to Radcliffe Road, and here turn left. At the end of the village turn left onto the fields, crossing diagonally on the waymarked footpath. Ignore the adjacent bridleway along the edge of the field.

In the far corner of the field, pass through the gateway and follow the hedge on your left. Ignore a stile on the left partway down the field – this leads back to the village and, if taken in reverse, represents a useful short cut from Back Lane.

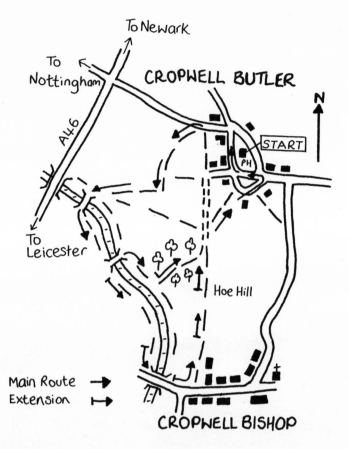

To Newark

To Nottingham

CROPWELL BUTLER

A46

START

PH

To Leicester

Hoe Hill

N

Main Route →
Extension ↦

CROPWELL BISHOP

Continue to the top of the field and on along the far hedge. Go straight ahead in the next field, following the hedge round in a right-angle turn, bearing left and then right a little at the end to reach a handgate on your right. Pass through the gate and follow the fence on your right to reach Cropwell Locks, where the Grantham Canal crossed the Fosse Way. There is a picnic site here, but whether or not you are picnicking, this is a delightful spot to rest awhile.

Doubling back along the embankment, cross the dry canal bed by a bridge and turn left along the former towpath.

For the optional extension, continue beside the canal bed as far as the road, at Cropwell Bishop. Turn left along the road, then left again between the memorial ground and a housing estate. Follow the bridleway through, re-joining the main route after Hoe Hill Wood.

The view beside Cropwell Locks.

For the main walk, at the next footbridge on the towpath, cross back and follow the adjacent hedge, and the edge of Hoe Hill Wood, to reach a stile. Cross the stile and follow the footpath through the wood. On reaching the far side, cross another stile and follow the hedge down the left of the field, turning left at the bottom into an enclosed lane.

Follow the lane as it ascends gently, ignoring a bridleway sign on your left. Take the next footpath on the right, crossing a stile and heading over the field to pass to the left of a row of houses and reach Back Lane. Follow the lane round, back to Main Street and the inn.

Places of interest nearby

The Wild Flower Farm Visitors Centre at Coach Gap Lane, Langar, is open from Friday to Sunday, and Bank Holiday Mondays, Easter to September inclusive.

To the east of Langar, just across the border in Leicestershire, is *Belvoir Castle*.

19 Ruddington
The Red Heart

The Red Heart is a typical, attractive village pub, and the oldest inn in the large south Nottinghamshire village of Ruddington. The basic form of the house has not altered significantly since the time of its farmhouse origins. The outside barns have been adapted to form the present-day cellar and store rooms, and there are still horse-tethering rings to be seen at the front of the building. The inn is believed to take its name from the Queen of Hearts, and is reported to be richly endowed with spirits – and not just the bottled variety. We are told there is the ghost of a little girl who died here, as well as that of a Cavalier soldier. And we are advised of the customer who once took a photograph inside the pub and is convinced that a shadowy 'presence' in the picture is that of a naked lady!

The inn belongs to Shipstone's Brewery (Greenalls) and the ales on offer include traditional handpumped varieties, such as Shipstone's, Tetley and Greenalls Original. Then there is Guinness, Mild, Carling and Labbatt's lagers, and Strongbow, Woodpecker and Scrumpy Jack cider. Wines are available by the glass or the bottle. The opening hours are from 11.30 am to 3 pm and 6.30 pm to 11 pm on Monday to Saturday. On Sunday the pub is open from 12 noon to 3 pm and 7 pm to 10.30 pm. At the time of our visit, food was available only at lunchtimes, but there were plans for an early introduction of evening catering. So do check. Popular specialities on the menu include Boozey Beef Pie, made from a secret recipe with lots of Guinness, home-made lasagne and Red Heart Country Loaf – a large hand-made roll with various hot or cold fillings. There is a different 'Chef's Special' on most days and a Friday roast in the carvery. A special Sunday menu – very popular – offers a choice of meat and vegetables, starters and home-made sweets (pre-booking is essential for this). Vegetarians will also find their needs fully catered for. On the snacks front, there is a staggering selection of filled country loaves or baps – highly recommended – Damon's jacket potatoes and Heidi's Stilton or Cheddar bites, to name just a few. Families are welcome at the Red Heart, and there is a family room, a children's play area and a beer garden. Dogs are also welcome if well-behaved, but only on a lead, and not inside at night.

Telephone 0115 9216453.

How to get there: Ruddington is just off the A60 Nottingham to Loughborough road, a mile or so to the south of the Nottingham ring road. If approaching from the south, take the next turning on the left after the Kirk Lane traffic lights (Easthorpe Street), and the Red Heart will be found on the right, just before reaching High Street. From the Nottingham direction, there is no right turn into Easthorpe Street, so you will need to turn right at the Kirk Lane lights and go round via High Street.

Ruddington village is served by Bartons and Nottingham City Transport, and the Trent Nottingham to Loughborough service follows the A60 road.

Parking: Customers are welcome to leave their vehicles here in the pub car park for the term of their walk. Alternative parking space is available on the old Loughborough road, just by the start of the bridleway – worth knowing if you fancy a slightly shorter route.

Length of the walk: 3¹/₂ miles. Maps: OS Landranger 129 Nottingham and Loughborough, Pathfinder 833 Long Eaton (inn GR 574332).

One of the most popular walks in the Ruddington area and a favourite of the author and his family, is the 'Nine Stiles' round. This is a two-stage walk, the first half being a pure bridlepath with no stiles at all. The second stage – the Nine Stiles proper – is a bit of a teaser. Try counting the stiles. You might make it nine, but we suspect you will find at least one of the nine surplus to requirements!

The Walk

Follow Easthorpe Street through to Loughborough Road and turn left. Just after the Esso garage, cross the road and, at the junction with the old Loughborough road, turn right between a pair of solid gateposts, following the waymarked bridleway – a broad farm lane, passing to the right of Ruddington Hall park. There is a good view of the hall – now used as offices – across the wide parkland. Beyond the hall grounds the track bends sharp left for Hall Farm. Keep straight ahead here until you reach a bungalow entrance, and then bear right, to continue along a grassy path on the left of the hedge. Follow the path through to the ring road.

The most direct route from here is along the road, to the right, but there is no proper footpath and, personally, I take no delight in following busy motor roads. A much pleasanter way is to cross over the road and go through a private car park, to reach Landmere Lane and Wheatcroft's Garden Centre. You might well enjoy a break here, browsing round the garden centre (refreshments available).

Follow the lane past the garden centre, to reach Melton Road, by the Lings Bar roundabout. Turn right here, and recross the ring road, continuing straight ahead along the minor road opposite, Flawforth Lane. Where the lane bends leftwards, by a stream, turn off right and cross a stile – the first of the 'nine' – following the waymarked path. Follow the left of the field until, near the far end, you reach a stile and footbridge on your left. Cross over the stream and turn right, continuing round the edge of the field to reach, and cross, a second (plank) bridge. Then turn right again, over a further plank bridge, to continue ahead on the left of the hedge.

As the hedge (and an accompanying track) bears to the right, keep to your existing line and reach a stile. The traditional route from here

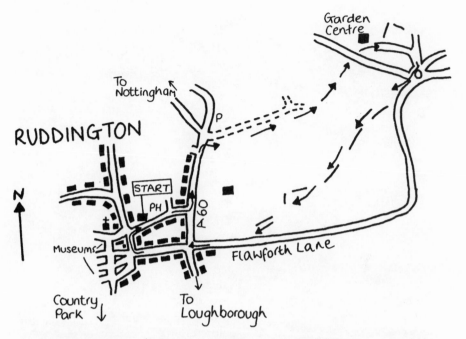

crosses the field on a diagonal line to reach the far fence, and there have been some attempts, it seems, to reinstate that line. There is, however, generally a growing crop in the field when we pass by, and no evidence of the crossing, and common practice favours the perimeter of the field.

If you follow this procedure, be sure to keep to the left of any temporary fence to reach a stile at the end of the field. This stile is topped with barbed wire and is not recommended, there being a much easier one further down the field, where the correct line of the path meets the fence. Cross over here, and then over four fields, bearing slightly left, to meet Flawforth Lane, close to the entrance to Silverdale Farm.

Turn right now, and cross the main road, continuing ahead along Kirk Lane, and round by High Street, back to Easthorpe Street and the inn.

Places of interest nearby
Ruddington has a brace of very interesting museums, both well worth an hour or two of your time. *The Village Museum* housed in St Peter's Rooms, Church Street, is open from Easter to late October,

Ruddington Bridleway.

on Sunday afternoons, and every afternoon in the months of July and August, except Mondays. *The Framework Knitters' Museum* in Chapel Street, is open Tuesday to Saturday from April to December, and on Bank Holiday Mondays.

The *Rushcliffe Country Park*, too, just off the Loughborough road, on the way to Bunny, is a lovely place to relax.

Bunny
The Rancliffe Arms

The inn at Bunny takes its name from Lord Rancliffe, a member of the Parkyns family, who were Lords of the Manor here for many generations. The village owes much of its flavour to the efforts of Sir Thomas Parkyns, 'the Wrestling Baronet', who provided many of the ancient and attractive buildings still gracing the place today – the hall, the vicarage, the almshouses and the old school. The inn itself dates back to the 17th century, and an interesting old structure in the centre of the car park, with pigeon holes in the gable, must surely be of similar vintage.

The Rancliffe is deservedly well known in the area as a traditional country pub with friendly staff, offering excellent real ale and good food in pleasant surroundings. One of Mansfield Brewery's houses, the range of ales includes Riding Bitter and Mild and Old Baily. Strongbow cider is available on draught, and McEwan's and Foster's lagers are both sold here. Opening hours are from 11.30 am to 2.30 pm and 6 pm to 11 pm, Monday to Saturday, and from 12 noon to 3 pm and 7 pm to 10.30 pm on Sunday.

The inn has its own large dining hall, or you can, if you wish, eat in the more relaxed atmosphere of the lounge or the cosy taproom with its ancient beams. Home-made food is served every lunchtime and in the evening, with the exception of Sunday and Monday evenings. There is a wide range of delicacies on offer, including steak and kidney pie, beef bourguignonne, chicken with barbecue sauce and vegetable lasagne, not to mention various fish dishes and grills, and a tempting selection of desserts to follow. Outside there is a beer garden. No special family room or play area is available but families are welcome. Well-behaved dogs can join you in the bar-room.
Telephone: 0115 9844727.

How to get there: Bunny lies halfway between Nottingham and Loughborough on the A60. The Rancliffe is a prominent building on the eastern side of the main road.

Buses calling at Bunny include the Trent service between Nottingham and Loughborough and Midland Fox buses from Coalville.

Parking: There is no objection to customers leaving their cars in the pub's car park while taking a walk.

Length of the walk: 3¹/₂ miles. Maps: OS Landranger 129 Nottingham and Loughborough, Pathfinder 853 Loughborough North and Castle Donington (inn GR 584296).

Bunny Hill, just to the south of this charming old village, used, it has been said, to be the despair of coachmen and early motorists. The gradient is easier today, and the internal combustion engine has likewise improved conditions, so that today's motorist dashes over the hill without a thought for the beauty around him. Not so we perambulists. A belt of woodland spans the hill on either side of the road – New Wood on the one side and Old Wood on the other. These woods are delightful at any time, but are particularly so when the bluebells are in flower.

The Walk
Cross the road and follow Main Street (not the main road, but the side road on the left of the church) through to its end, at a stile. Bear left over the stile, crossing the field diagonally to reach and go over